an introduction to the soul

a trilogy comprising the little book of the soul, your holographic soul & the future of the soul

ian lawton

First published as a trilogy in 2010 by Rational Spirituality Press comprising:

The Little Book of the Soul, Third Edition, 2010.
Your Holographic Soul, First Edition, 2010.
The Future of the Soul, First Edition, 2010.

All enquiries to be directed to www.rspress.org.

Copyright © Ian Lawton 2007, 2008, 2010. All rights reserved.

The rights of Ian Lawton to be identified as the Author of the Work have been asserted by him in accordance with the Copyright, Designs and Patents Act 1988.

No part of this book may be used or reproduced in any manner whatsoever (excluding brief quotations embodied in critical articles and reviews), nor by way of trade or otherwise be lent, resold, hired out, or otherwise circulated in any form of binding or cover other than that in which it is published, without the publisher's prior written consent.

A CIP catalogue record for this title is available from the British Library.

ISBN 978-0-9549176-7-8

Cover design by Ian Lawton.
Cover image by Jason Waskey (www.jasonwaskey.com).
Author photograph by Gaia Giakali.

the little book of the soul
true stories that could change your life

ian lawton

the crying baby	2
hotel california	4
the gi joe dolls	7
the 1200 rupees	10
the chateau	16
the buried flagstone	20
the hall of records	28
the guilt that wouldn't go	34
a personal story	41

The aim of this little book isn't merely to preach to the converted. It's equally if not more aimed at those who have no fixed views about religion or spirituality, and probably don't even have much time to think about such things.

So whether you're young or old, rich or poor, believer or non-believer, this little book is for you.

It's so confusing, isn't it? Why are we all here? What is life for? And who is best placed to tell us?

We've got religion on one side, telling us that we'll survive death and maybe get judged and maybe go to heaven or hell. It gives some people a lot of hope. But others just see how different preachers try to tell us what to do, based on what various prophets may or may not have said thousands of years ago; and how religion tends to divide rather than unite, providing the excuse for countless wars and conflicts. Perhaps we just feel that enough is enough.

Now, we've also got science on the other side, telling us it's all a load of nonsense, and that when we die, we die. They are intelligent people, and their arguments sound so sensible. And anyway, isn't this rational approach just what we need to stop all the killing and bloodshed?

But what about those of us who feel a deep unease when scientists tell us that the physical world around us is all there is? Even more important, is this just because we are so stupid that we need to believe in something more? Or is it because our intuition is literally crying out that they're wrong?

If so, where does this leave the huge numbers of us who strongly suspect there is something more, but are rational and logical and want to see proper evidence and argument? Up until now religion and spirituality have always relied on faith and belief, leaving science to occupy the rational, intellectual high ground.

But is there now reliable, modern evidence that makes it possible to turn all this on its head – and combine the words rational and spirituality in a sensible, meaningful way? And can we for the first time develop a spiritual way of thinking that is properly grounded in evidence, not faith?

the crying baby

George Rodonaia had a difficult childhood in Soviet Russia. His parents were murdered when he was very young, and he was adopted by a family from Georgia who showered him with love and made sure he received a first-class education. But then they both died of cancer, within three years of each other, and at the tender age of twelve he was left alone in their home to fend for himself.

George realized he would have to work hard, and he applied himself to his studies with vigor. His big break came when an essay of his was published in the University of Moscow newspaper. It caught the eye of the president, who liked it so much he invited him to attend, even though he was only fourteen. He soon developed into a gifted medical research scientist.

In 1974, at the age of eighteen, he was invited to study at Yale. He was delighted at this recognition of his talents, and at the opportunities it would open up. But the KGB had other ideas. He was researching the way certain chemicals acted on the human brain, and they found this useful for interrogations. If they could not keep him, they did not want the US to have him either.

Over the next two years they put various obstacles in his way but, when he got married and had a child, it finally appeared they would let him leave. Then on the day of his departure, as he stood on the pavement in Tbilisi waiting for a taxi to the airport, he was mown down by a car and pronounced dead at the scene. Bystanders confirmed that, having already sent George flying, the driver had even reversed back to run over him again.

His body lay in a morgue for three days. But as the autopsy began his eyelids flickered, and he was rushed to surgery. Naturally his family and friends were amazed and overjoyed at his survival. But that was only the beginning of a much stranger journey for them all.

As a man of science, George had never had any time for religion: 'I was very much a typical young research scientist and a pretty skeptical one, too. I was not religious at all. I was an atheist. I had basically accepted the materialistic perspective of the hard sciences that everything can and should be reduced to a material cause. There was no room for spirituality for me at all; out of the question, totally out of the question.'

So those close to him were bewildered when, three days into his lengthy recovery, he began to describe what had happened to him while he was 'dead'. He claimed that he had been surrounded by a bright, white light that radiated a sense of peace and joy, and that his whole life had flashed in front of him in an instant of pure understanding. He even claimed that he had been able to travel back to any period in history, and experience it exactly as if he was there, just by thinking about it. Had the trauma he suffered driven him mad?

These doubts mounted when George claimed that he had also been able to travel anywhere he liked while 'out of body'. In particular he was drawn to the newborn daughter of a neighbor. She remained in the hospital in which his body lay because she would not stop crying, and doctors had been unable to diagnose the problem. But much to his surprise he found that he was able to communicate with her telepathically, even though the surrounding adults remained blissfully unaware of his presence. What is more, he was somehow able to scan her body and establish that her hip had been broken at birth.

Incredibly, as soon as George was able to pass on this information, the doctors x-rayed the baby and found that she did indeed have a fractured hip. But how could he have made such an accurate diagnosis while his physical body was lying in a mortuary cabinet? And, even more worryingly for any skeptic, if *this* part of his story was true, what about all the rest of it?

So profound was his experience that, once fully recovered, George threw himself into spiritual study and became ordained as a church minister. He moved to the US in 1989, and in 1996 founded the first international congress on spiritual enlightenment hosted by the United Nations in New York.

Sadly a massive heart attack ended his life prematurely in 2004. But not before he had been able to share his story freely, and to inspire thousands of people through talks and radio broadcasts.

hotel california

In 1991 doctors told Pam Reynolds, a 35-year-old musician from Atlanta, Georgia, that she had very little time to live: 'They gave me virtually no chance of survival. I will never forget the terrible sadness that permeated the air as my husband drove to our attorney's office for the filing of my last will and testament. Somehow, we would have to tell our three small children that, soon, Mommy would make the journey to heaven, leaving them with the few, short memories their tender years could afford them.'

Pam's problem was that a blood vessel at the base of her brain had ballooned into an aneurysm, and death was the most likely result whether her doctors operated or not. Only one man just might be able to save her.

In Phoenix, Arizona, Dr Robert Spetzler had pioneered a procedure called 'standstill'. Pam's body temperature would be reduced until her heart stopped, then the operating table would be lifted at one end so the blood could drain from her head. He would have about half an hour to fix the problem before her brain would suffer permanent damage from lack of oxygen.

Much to everyone's relief the operation was a complete success. But there was more. Not long after she came round she reported that she had left her body during surgery. She said she had entered a tunnel and then emerged into an intense, bright light, where she was greeted by her beloved grandmother and other deceased family members. Apparently they projected an incredible, 'sparkly' energy into her, and part of her wanted to go into the light with them. But without words they conveyed that if she did she would be changed, and unable to return. So, with young children to raise, and despite some reluctance, she agreed to go back down the tunnel. Her body, still lying on the operating table, felt cold and heavy as she was propelled back in.

Was all this merely her imagination? It seems unlikely, because there is yet more to Pam's story. She also reported on a number of things that were happening in the operating theatre at the time. She said that when she had first floated out of her body she had seen herself lying on the operating table below: 'It was the most aware that I think that I have ever been in my entire life... It was brighter and more focused and clearer than normal vision.'

One detail she remembered was one of the doctors discussing the fact that her arteries were too small. And they subsequently confirmed that they had had trouble inserting the tubes into her inner thighs that would hook up to the bypass machine to cool her blood.

But does this prove anything? We know that she had small speaker-plugs fitted into her ears at the beginning of the operation, to emit regular pulses to check on her brainstem reaction. Yet skeptics suggest that she would still have been able to hear through these, especially if her anesthetic levels were low at the beginning and end of the operation.

They may be right in this. But there is one other element of Pam's recall that cannot be explained away so simply, because it involves sight rather than hearing. She described how, when she first floated out of her body, she also saw Dr Spetzler handling the saw used to open her skull. She said it was shaped like an 'electric toothbrush', with a 'groove in the top', and even commented on the other blades housed in what looked like a 'socket wrench case' by the side.

Again the medical staff were subsequently able to confirm that her detailed description was indeed accurate, even though they were astonished that it came from someone with no medical training. Nor, they said, could she have seen the instrument at the beginning of the operation, because it would have been surgically sealed and hidden away.

Let us be clear that at this point in the operation Pam was fully unconscious, and her anesthetic levels should have been high, even if she would only be clinically dead a little later. Even more crucially, her eyelids had been greased and taped shut right at the start. So how could she 'see' so accurately without the normal use of her eyes?

Pam too has shared her experience widely, especially via her music. She knows that it was not her time to leave – in particular because of the song she heard playing as she returned to her body, which the cleanup team later confirmed had been playing at the end of the operation. It was 'Hotel California' by the Eagles. Indeed she found it particularly ironic that the lyric was 'you can check out any time you like, but you can never leave'.

'Near-death' experiences like these have massive implications. Of course skeptics might suggest that George's and Pam's reports of the 'light' resulted from a mixture of chemicals playing tricks on the brain and vivid imagination. But their memories were lucid and detailed, and are consistent with thousands of similar cases – as well as with other, completely different types of experience that we've yet to discuss.

More crucially still, dismissing them as mere hallucinations doesn't even attempt to account for the verifiable and obscure details that people like this have brought back from their experiences. And as we'll see there are many similar cases in other areas of research where information obtained by unusual means proves not only accurate, but also highly unlikely to have come from pure guesswork or coincidence – because in no sense is it 'obvious'.

The other 'normal' explanation for such impressive cases would have to be deliberate fraud, with the motive of gaining attention and even fame. But is this really likely to apply to a young man like George, who already had a scientific reputation to protect and foster? Or to Pam, who'd surely have little desire to trick people having just survived against all the odds?

What's more, those who come forward often risk ridicule and worse from skeptics. But speak out they do, because they know their reports of other realms are important.

Nor can these experiences be dismissed out of hand as mere hearsay or anecdote. As with most of the other reports we'll look at later, they have been thoroughly recorded and investigated by professionals – that is, fully qualified doctors, psychologists or psychiatrists.

So what do such near-death experiences tell us? They surely suggest strongly that we have a consciousness that survives intact without the physical brain and body. We might even go as far as to call it a soul.

This provides us with our first key proposition:

the soul survives independent of the physical body

But does a soul have just one life on earth, or many?

the gi joe dolls

From the earliest age James Leininger of Lafayette, Louisiana had been fascinated with aircraft. He spent hours playing with toy planes, and always pointed and yelled when he saw a real aircraft in the sky.

His parents Bruce and Andrea, a well-educated and grounded couple, were both satisfied that this was just typical childhood behavior – even when James became obsessed with crashing his planes into the living room table that served as his landing strip. But in the spring of 2000, as he approached his second birthday, vivid nightmares began. He would regularly thrash around in his sleep, especially kicking out with his legs up in the air. And it was the words he uttered while writhing that really shook his parents: 'Airplane crash, on fire, little man can't get out.'

They began to fear that his obsession might not be so harmless after all. Why on earth did he keep replaying the actions of a pilot desperately trying to kick out his cockpit window? It was at this point that Andrea's mother, having read a book about similar cases, suggested that these might be memories of a past life. Andrea contacted the author, Carol Bowman, and followed her suggestion that she and Bruce should take the nightmares seriously and discuss them with James.

This did reduce their regularity. But as a result James also started to come up with startling details, usually when being comforted after a nightmare. Over that summer and into the autumn he revealed that the pilot of the plane was also called James; that he had been shot down by the Japanese; that he had flown Corsairs; and that one of his fellow pilots went by the name of Jack Larsen. He also mysteriously mentioned the single word *Natoma*.

Bruce remained dubious about any sort of spiritual explanation, but his curiosity simply would not allow him to ignore the level of detail James was reporting. He knew that neither he nor any other member of their family had any particular interest in aircraft or the war. Nor did he feel that the information could have come from such a young child, who could not even read at this point, watching documentaries without anyone else being aware of it. So, still with the primary intention of somehow proving that there was a perfectly rational explanation for James' memories, he began to research them.

His first port of call was to search for the word *Natoma* on the internet. This quickly established that an aircraft carrier called the USS *Natoma Bay* had been stationed in the Pacific during the latter part of

World War II and, among other things, had taken part in the notorious battle for the Japanese island of Iwo Jima early in 1945. Coincidentally his book club catalogue included one all about this battle, so he ordered it, even though at this point he still felt the whole thing was pure coincidence.

But not long afterwards he was really shell-shocked for the first time. One day he was flicking through the book when James came over to sit on his lap, and it happened to be open at a map. Immediately James pointed to the island of Chichi Jima to the north of Iwo Jima and said, 'Daddy, that is where my plane was shot down.'

His interest now well and truly piqued, Bruce continued his internet research and came across a 'Natoma Bay Association', by which means he was able to contact a radioman who had been involved in the Iwo Jima conflict. And although he reported that their squadron had flown only Avengers and Wildcats, not Corsairs, he did confirm that a Jack Larsen had been one of the pilots. This was starting to look like more than just coincidence.

For the next eighteen months Bruce searched military records trying to find out more details about Larsen, but in vain. Indeed he was close to giving up when he attended a reunion of the Natoma Bay Association in the autumn of 2002. Without disclosing his real interest, he was able to establish that Larsen was not dead as he had assumed, but alive and living in Arkansas. Even more revealing, he found out that while a total of twenty-one men had been lost from the *Natoma Bay* during the campaign in the Pacific, only one pilot had been lost at Chichi Jima – and coincidentally his name was Lt *James* M Huston Jr. Aged only twenty-one, he had volunteered to fly that one last mission on 3 March 1945 before he was due to return to the US.

Bruce immediately arranged to visit Larsen in Arkansas, and he confirmed he had been Huston's wingman that day. But neither he nor any other members of the squadron had actually seen what happened to Huston's plane in the heat of battle.

Nevertheless, something else now slotted into place for the increasingly stunned Bruce. His son had always signed his drawings of aircraft 'James 3'. Was this his way of recognizing that his former personality had been James Huston *Junior*, and his father in turn James Huston *Senior*?

At this point the investigation switched to tracking down any surviving members of the deceased's family, and at the beginning of 2003 Bruce made contact with Huston's elderly sister, Anne Barron, in California. Without telling her his true interest they became friendly, and she kindly sent him a number of packages of photos of her long-departed brother.

By this time the only major statement that James had made that did not ring true was his insistence that his former personality had flown Corsairs. Bruce knew that Huston had been flying a Wildcat on that fateful day, and this gave him some sort of faint hope that James' memories might still turn out to be just coincidental. That was until he examined the photographs – because in amongst them was a clear shot of Huston standing proudly next to a Corsair.

Bruce subsequently confirmed from military records that, before he was posted to the *Natoma Bay*, Huston had been part of an elite special squadron of only twenty pilots, the 'Devil's Disciples', who test-flew Corsairs for carrier use. At this point he finally submitted to what his wife and others had long accepted – that his son James really was the reincarnation of a pilot who had died nearly sixty years before.

But even this was not all, because James made a number of other detailed and obscure statements that turned out to be true. For example, he insisted that Corsairs often suffered with tire punctures, which was confirmed by an aircraft museum. He also said that his former personality's plane had been shot in the engine, which set it on fire before it hit the sea. And eventually Bruce made contact with several members of a bomber squadron that had also been attacking Chichi Jima that day, who all confirmed that they had seen the engine on Huston's plane explode into flame.

As if his detailed recall of names, places and other obscure information were not enough, perhaps the most impressive part of James' recall related to three 'GI Joe' dolls that he called Leon, Walter and Billie. Again military records confirmed that three of the pilots from Huston's squadron who had been killed in other *Natoma Bay* engagements were Lt *Leon* S Conner, Ensign *Walter* J Devlin and Ensign *Billie* R Peeler.

In fact when James was asked why he named the dolls that way he replied, 'Because they greeted me when I went to heaven.' The records also showed that all three had died before Huston.

In an entirely fitting conclusion James is now, once again, in possession of two of his former personality's most treasured belongings, forwarded on by the military after Huston's death and in turn by his sister Anne when she heard the rest of the story: a bust of George Washington, and a model of a Corsair aircraft.

the 1200 rupees

Madhya Pradesh is a huge, central state in India. It was here that Swarnlata Mishra was born in 1948 – and she was only three years old when she began to reveal amazing details of another life.

On this occasion her father – an inspector of schools – had decided to take her on a trip from their home city of Panna in the north of the state to the central city of Jabalpur, some 170 miles to the south. On their return they were less than a third of the way home when, on the outskirts of the city of Katni, Swarnlata asked the driver to turn down a road towards 'my house'. Shortly afterwards, when they had stopped for a meal in Katni, she again insisted that they would obtain much better food in *her* house nearby.

Of course this puzzled her father, but it was not until some time later that he discovered she was continuing to talk about her previous life in Katni to her brothers and sisters. She said her name had been Biya Pathak.

A number of years passed, during which time Swarnlata and her family moved some forty miles west to the district of Chhatarpur so that her father could take up a new post. Every now and then she would refer to her past life, but it was not until she was ten years old that he started to take her more seriously.

The breakthrough came when a local professor, having heard a vague rumor about Swarnlata's claims, invited her and her father to dinner. During the meal Swarnlata learned that the professor's wife originally came from Katni, and asked to meet her. Swarnlata's recognition of an old friend of Biya's was instant. And the lady herself was stunned when Swarnlata reminded her of how, in her former life, they had had difficulty in finding a toilet at a wedding in the village of Tilora.

Could a child's vivid imagination alone really come up with such detailed information? Unlikely. Although this time it is not of a historical nature, once again it is not only verifiable but also highly obscure. And certainly the *extent* of information provided by Swarnlata seems to make guesswork statistically impossible, as we are about to see.

For the first time her father now documented the key statements she had made to date, including that Biya had had two sons, and that her family had owned a motor car – a rarity in this part of India even by the 1950s. She especially recalled a number of details about her former home. Apparently it was white on the outside, with black front doors fitted with iron bars for security. Inside there were four decoratively plastered rooms, while others were less well finished, and the front of the house had stone floor slabs. Behind it lay a girls' school, while a railway line and lime furnaces were also nearby.

Katni is well known as one of the largest railway junctions in India, and also for its lime deposits, so the last two statements might be regarded as easy guesses if Swarnlata were making it all up. But what about the other less obvious details?

Not long after the incident at the professor's house the leading Indian paranormal researcher, Hemendra Banerjee, learned of the case, and he spent two days with Swarnlata and her family in their home in Chhatarpur. He was so impressed that he made up his mind to go to Katni to try to locate her former family. But he knew that Pathak was an extremely common name in the region, so he would only have her statements about her former home to guide him.

Nonetheless in time he was able to find a house that matched the external description, in the right location near to a school, railway and lime furnaces. And the family who owned the house was well known in the Katni-Jabalpur area for their extensive business interests, and were indeed called Pathak. So far so good. But in his wildest dreams Banerjee could not have expected to find that they did indeed have a deceased daughter called Biya. After her marriage she had moved to Maihar, a town some forty miles to the north, where she and her husband had raised two sons. But unfortunately she had died in 1939 from heart disease.

This alone ought to be enough to convince most skeptics. But in fact it was only the beginning of an even more extraordinary case.

In that same summer of 1959 several members of Biya's family decided to visit Chhatarpur to test Swarnlata out. First her eldest brother arrived unannounced at the Mishra family home, but Swarnlata quickly recognized him and called him by the nickname Biya had used, 'Babu'. Then, in conjunction with Swarnlata's father, Biya's widowed husband and one of her sons arranged a meeting in which they were anonymously present amongst nine other local men. Not only did Swarnlata identify them both, but she did so despite Biya's son trying to throw her off the scent for a full twenty-four hours. He insisted that he was someone else, and that a friend he had brought along was Biya's other son. But on both counts Swarnlata stuck to her guns, quite correctly.

Not long afterwards Swarnlata traveled to Katni to visit her former home for the first time. Here she correctly identified a number of people without any leading, and even, again, with a certain amount of deliberate *mis*leading. These included Biya's other three brothers and various other relations; a Pathak family servant; the family cowherd – refusing to be put off by claims that she was wrong because he was dead; and a former family friend and his wife – commenting on his spectacles, which he had not worn when Biya was alive. She also asked about a neem tree in the compound and a parapet at the back of the house, both of which had been there in Biya's time but were now missing.

Further visits to Katni and Maihar followed in which more people were recognized and statements verified, up to a total of nearly fifty in all. But perhaps the most compelling piece of evidence came from Swarnlata confiding to her former husband that he had taken 1200 rupees from Biya's money box. This was something of an embarrassment that, he confirmed, had been known only to himself and his former wife.

Faced with such overwhelming evidence, it was not long before all parties fully accepted the reality that Swarnlata was Biya reincarnate. Indeed she continued to visit her former family regularly, and their close bonds were re-established. What amazed onlookers was the way that, in the company of her former brothers, she would adopt the attitude of an older sister. And they in turn seemed to accept this as perfectly reasonable – despite the fact that in this life she was their junior by some forty years.

So what do skeptics have to say about apparent past-life memories like these? One normal explanation offered for many cases is that the children involved were combining vivid imagination with information learned normally by overhearing conversations, or from television and radio programs and so on – albeit that their parents remained unaware of, or had forgotten about, these possible influences.

This might seem to work if the families were reasonably close to each other and the murder or death of the 'previous' person was locally notorious. But that certainly wasn't true of the two cases above, in which the children also came up with detailed information that only a handful of people, or even only one other individual, knew about. Nor do skeptics offer any convincing explanation as to why so many children identify with these lives as their own, if they've merely overheard other people talking about them.

What other normal explanations are there? On the face of it, in this area of research it's rather more likely that the children's parents might have deliberately and fraudulently 'coached' them for potential financial reward – especially if the previous family was somewhat wealthier. But this would give the latter every reason to be suspicious and uncooperative – and was almost certainly why the Pathak's initially gave Swarnlata such a hard time. Not only that, but it's clear that in some cases the child remembers a less well-off former life. While in others the current family actively discourages contact with the former family for a long time – especially when they've already been bombarded with comments about their child's 'other mother or father', and are already scared of having to compete for their child's affections.

And, again, we're not just dealing with anecdotes. Most of these children's cases have been investigated by professionals – in particular the team set up by Dr Ian Stevenson, the former head of psychiatry at the University of Virginia, who dedicated his life to this research. They've developed detailed protocols to check for normal transmission of information, and fraud, and since the early 1960s have collated what are now over three thousand cases from all over the world.

Skeptics have questioned some aspects of these protocols, and indeed not only Stevenson's impartiality but that of some of his assistants as well. They've also managed to pick holes in a couple of his cases, and to argue that they should have been recognized as fraudulent. All of this isn't without a certain justification. But to then suggest that the motive for fraud was widespread in his cases, and confidently announce that every single one can be explained by normal means, is going way too far, as detailed analysis shows.

Above all they deliberately ignore cases like those of James and Swarnlata. Not only did these two come up with incredibly obscure information, but their current families weren't particularly poor, and no credible motive for fraud has been shown. So the selective and simplistic dismissals of skeptics just will not do.

But even if we accept some sort of paranormal or spiritual explanation, do these cases necessarily indicate that we have many lives? What if, for example, these children were somehow tapping into some sort of 'universal memory bank'? This seems unlikely, because in most cases their recollections aren't just impassive but produce intense emotions, sometimes pleasurable and sometimes painful, such as James' nightmares. Often, too, they display the strong behavioral traits of the past personality.

Alternatively, could they have been possessed by the disgruntled spirit of the former personality? This would better account for the depth of emotions and unusual behavioral traits. And the fact that the memories tend to fade between the ages of five and nine would arguably correspond to the suggestion that children tend to be more susceptible to possession. But a number of these children briefly mention how they 'hung around' after their death, until they decided to pick some new parents and be born again. This seems to indicate a certain individual continuity from one life to the next.

So it would appear that the best explanation for these cases is that the children are recalling their own individual lives, not anyone else's.

Intriguingly there's equally strong evidence of past lives from another area of research, even though it's often written off as being subjective and unreliable – even sometimes by those who accept the idea of reincarnation. And that's the regression of adults into their past lives, whether by hypnosis or other means.

Most professional psychologists and psychiatrists have a largely scientific training, which tends even now to encourage skepticism about any kind of spiritual dimension. Yet from the middle of the last century an increasing number of such professionals around the globe found that occasionally patients would appear to regress into past lives without prompting. And those brave enough to 'think outside the box' became increasingly convinced that these experiences couldn't just be dismissed. After all, they wouldn't dismiss memories arising from normal regression into childhood, which uses exactly the same technique.

In fact those who actively experimented with past-life therapy found that the results could be incredible. Serious problems that might have resisted years of conventional therapy were sometimes permanently alleviated within only a few sessions. It even seemed that the therapy worked whether or not the participants believed in reincarnation. But the pioneering therapists found themselves sufficiently convinced that they risked their professional reputations by going into print on the subject.

Of course no sensible person would suggest that all past-life memories retrieved by regression are entirely historically accurate. It's perfectly possible for imagination and normally acquired information – whether consciously remembered or not – to combine to create a fascinating and apparently authentic story that doesn't represent a past life at all.

But we've seen that the crucial factor in near-death and children's past-life cases is the recall of detailed and obscure facts that can be subsequently verified. So are there any similarly impressive regression cases?

The story of Australian psychologist Peter Ramster is broadly typical of the pattern described above. In the early 1970s he set up a hypnotherapy practice in Sydney and, despite initial skepticism, became increasingly intrigued by the fragments of his patients' past lives that kept emerging. And he too discovered that these could deliver impressive therapeutic results.

For most therapists this is enough, and they don't feel the need to question the authenticity or otherwise of the experience. But Ramster's insatiable curiosity wouldn't allow him to leave it at that. Instead he decided to experiment with his subjects, in a concentrated attempt to elicit detailed factual information that could be checked.

Luckily for posterity, film-making was his favorite hobby. So after a decade of diligent research he was in a position to put his own film crew together, and to take several of his best subjects halfway across the world – to Europe, the setting for the past lives in question. He wanted to see if their detailed recall under hypnosis in Australia matched the facts on the ground.

So, how did they get on?

the chateau

Amelie de Cheville was the daughter of a wealthy French merchant. They owned a chateau to the northwest of the market town of Flers in Normandy. She grew up alongside her brother Philippe, their every whim attended to by servants, watching with amazement and envy as the beautifully dressed guests arrived for an endless procession of lavish balls. Often these were held by the lake in the grounds of the estate, and minstrels played on as the guests danced long into the night.

But the carefree days of youth could not last forever. Before long she found herself marrying an army officer, and leaving the family home to move to a house on the Rue St George in Paris. She was still comfortably off, with servants of her own, but life was not quite as lavish as it had been with her father. She had two children, Edouarde and Marianne.

As time went on, life became increasingly difficult. The pressure for revolution was building as the gulf between rich and poor widened. Amelie decided to send her children, by now in their mid-teens, to the chateau for their safety. She rarely left the security of her home to venture into the streets of Paris, and when she did she found the streets filthy and overwhelmed by rats.

Then came the fateful day when she was dragged from her house by the mob and thrown into a small, dark cell. Nor was it long before she found herself being forced into a cart. Her hair had been cut short at the back, and she knew what was to come, but first she had to face the crowd on the journey to the square and their hatred left her numb with fear.

She watched as the victims ahead of her met their fate. So great was the bloodlust of the crowd that as soon as one head had fallen they were ready for the next. Every available vantage point was taken, every window and balcony, like some great sporting occasion. The heads were trophies to be stuck on spikes, while the bodies were flung over a wall and left to rot. The streets were literally rivers of blood.

Finally Amelie's turn came. She stumbled up the steps to the guillotine – confused, petrified, jostled and pulled from all sides. Her hands were tied behind her back, and as she was pushed down into position her throat struck the block so hard she nearly choked. Then, staring into the basket, with everything covered in a thick blanket of glistening blood, she heard the final 'swoosh'.

Little did she know that 200 years later she would be back in France, searching for traces of that life.

This was the most detailed of a number of lives that Cynthia Henderson described to Ramster while in trance in Australia, over the course of a number of sessions. It was enough to convince him to take her to France to see if they could find her former home. But it was a big risk, because none of them had even been there before, at least not in *this* life. However they would be aided by a young French Catholic with little sympathy for reincarnation called Antoine le Breton, who would act as the independent witness.

Starting from the bustling marketplace in Flers they followed the route she had described in trance: 'You go past the church for a while, and then you come to a road, a big road that goes between Rouen and St Michel. Go right there for about an hour [by coach], and then it starts to go up after you leave Flers, the road goes over the top of a hill. You can look down mainly on the left side, you can see woods, trees and fields... Then you turn left down to the chateau.'

Coming out of the town past the church and finding the main road north was no great problem, and before long they came to a long incline. At the top there was a spectacular view over a wooded valley on the left, and at the bottom a turning to the left, all just as Cynthia had described.

The smaller road wound around for a while and then, disaster! A new estate had been built, and the roads had changed completely. They could not go in the direction she wanted, so was this to be the end?

Fortunately after asking for directions they were able to pick up the original road on the other side of the estate, and before long she pointed excitedly to a long wall running alongside the road. She was convinced it belonged to the chateau, and that the entrance lay just ahead. As they drove into what was now a public park and slowly made their way up the tree-lined driveway, Cynthia's tension mounted: 'Oh God! I can't look... Oh God, there it is... It's a *tower*!' Previously it had been a tantalizing dream, but now it was a reality, and the emotion was too much. Cynthia began to sob deeply. She at least felt she had come home.

The chateau was a derelict ruin now after suffering bomb damage during the war, but it was not difficult to imagine its former splendor. Two stories high and crafted from cut sandstone blocks; the large porch with huge doors and long windows on each side; the imposing tower at the rear that she and her brother had been forbidden to climb; the lake nearby. All was exactly as she had described it in trance.

Once she had had time to get over the initial shock, they walked around and she soon found everything flooding back to her: 'I feel fantastic here. I feel as if I belong. It's incredible. I recognize everywhere... I have all these images of the coaches and the clothes and the people, the servants and the parties and everything, the whole bit... It's only just now that the impact has hit me, how real those people were, and this was my life! It's all so real to me. It's sort of like a big tunnel being opened up and my whole memory being brought back.'

The team then took her to Paris to see if they could locate her house there. This time she could not lead them from the outskirts because the environment had changed beyond recognition, but when they arrived at the Rue St George she knew where to look. Unfortunately the building at the site of her former home was completely different. And given her unpleasant memories of this latter part of her life, which were in such stark contrast to those of the chateau, the team agreed not to linger.

Nevertheless they had rather more success in tracing a regular holiday destination she had described as being within a few miles of the picturesque Mont St Michel, on the coast some fifty miles to the west of Flers. This was a large country house that she said had been owned by a friend of Amelie's father.

As the team left the car park at Mont St Michel they were once again relying on the clarity of Cynthia's recall. And this time she had said little about the journey in trance, so they were instead relying on her recognizing the route consciously as they went along. But they need not have worried, because the country roads had not changed too much and she retraced her steps as if it had been only yesterday. She directed them to take a number of turns, without making a single mistake. Then she told them they were approaching a stream, and that their goal was coming up on the right just around a bend – which it was. Again emotion got the better of her and she burst into tears.

Cynthia had described the house itself back in Australia, and the details were borne out when they pulled into the courtyard of a u-shaped mansion, with a central archway through which coaches would once have passed. The only difference was that a well lay in the centre of the courtyard rather than the fountain she had described, but even this could have been the one feature to have changed significantly in the intervening centuries.

As the team walked around Cynthia again felt her surroundings coming to life. She was particularly captivated by the chapel in the grounds of the house, which she had also described previously. Apart from many other details that could perhaps be put down to intelligent guesswork, she had reported that it had a hexagonal stone font on the left, dark wooden pews and, even more obscure, diamond-shaped blue-grey tiles on the floor. And, when the team obtained permission to enter the chapel, yet again all these details proved to be accurate.

This was the initially skeptical le Breton's reaction: 'It is difficult to work it out. It is a fascinating and intriguing experiment. It has reached the limit of credibility. It's absolutely different, I can't understand it. There is something spiritual at the heart of it.'

Remember, too, that all of these events were documented on film by Ramster and his team. In fact they had already investigated another case that was equally if not more impressive in England, to which we will now turn.

the buried flagstone

When Gwen McDonald first arrived in Ramster's office she had only come to provide moral support for a friend, who wanted to see if she could experience a past life under hypnosis. Gwen herself was a down-to-earth, middle-aged woman who had no belief in reincarnation at this time, and no desire to be regressed, so when Ramster said he could just as easily work with both of them to see how well they reacted she was initially reluctant.

Nevertheless after some persuasion she agreed, and how grateful we should be that she did because she turned out to be one of his finest subjects. She regressed easily and, albeit with some further reluctance that Ramster had to overcome, agreed to return to help with his ongoing research.

Initially he uncovered ten different past lives with her, which took place in various parts of the world, with the earliest as far back as prehistoric times. But for research purposes he decided that the most promising was a life in eighteenth-century England, a country that again Gwen had never visited in this life – indeed she had never even held a passport.

In trance she initially revealed that her name in this life was Rose Duncan, and that she lived with her father Adam and stepmother Bessie in a small dwelling called 'Rose Cottage', which was part of a larger estate. Although she did not say where this was, it is obvious to anyone just reading Ramster's written transcripts that when she became Rose she talked with a broad Somerset brogue.

The full details of this life then emerged over the course of a number of subsequent sessions. She was born in 1765, and had a happy and relatively uneventful childhood – although she later found out that at birth she had been taken away from her real mother, whose maiden name was Lethbridge, who was married to a Lord Somerville, and with whom her father had had an affair. He went away for long periods so she was mainly left with Bessie, of whom she was very fond, and Dobbs, Bessie's grandfather, who kept her entertained with many local tales and legends.

The highlight of her week was when she crossed fields and a stream to visit the nearest village to buy provisions, where she could look in the shops and meet local people.

She knew that the master of 'the big 'ouse' was called James Mackenzie, and that he owned various ships that traded around the globe. But he had taken the estate over from a Lord Panmure of Forth, a friend of her father's who was very kind to her when she was young. So she was less fond of Mackenzie, and even less of his annoying son Nicholas. Apparently he chased her for amusement when she was a girl, and for entirely different reasons as she developed into a young woman.

But her greatest pleasure was reserved for when she could walk right through the woods and fields and on to the ruins of the abbey at Glastonbury, which she reckoned to be some six miles away. Sadly, it also proved to be her ultimate undoing.

As she approached the age of eighteen her father began to cast about for a suitable husband. Mackenzie, Lord Panmure and her father were all expatriate Scotsmen – indeed it seems the latter had come to Somerset to hide away in the aftermath of the failed Jacobite rebellion of 1745. In any case, when he returned one day he announced that he had found a suitable candidate from the clan McCrae, and that after their marriage she would go to live in Scotland for good.

Rose was thrown into confusion. The poor girl did not want to leave the home and people she loved, and was not at all sure she was ready to be married, especially not to a complete stranger. Worse still, the McRae's were relatives of the Mackenzies – who by this time Rose had come to hate with a passion.

Desperately confused and scared she ran for miles until she reached the abbey, her favorite place when she needed time to think, but as night started to close in it was too late to try to make her way home. Gradually the temperature dropped and the cold became more intense, so she took refuge in one of the ruined buildings and huddled up in a corner to fight off the cold as best she could.

Her parents had no idea where to look until they asked Dobbs, who knew of Rose's love for the abbey, but by the time they found her it was morning and she was already very ill. They took her home on their cart, and Bessie nursed her in bed. But after several weeks she succumbed to pneumonia and died.

Gwen's life as Rose became Ramster's 'lead' case because it was so rich in detail. But before he could commit to taking her and others halfway around the world, he needed to do some preliminary checking of the accuracy or otherwise of Rose's story. He and a colleague devoted hours to poring over old records in the New South Wales Library, and it proved well worth the effort.

He had specifically asked Rose to name the villages in the surrounding area, and the majority of these checked out on modern maps as clustered together in southeast Somerset. Langport, Somerton, Alford, East and West Pennard, West Bradley and Croscombe – which she correctly pronounced 'Crocom' – were all there within about a twelve-mile radius of each other. Better still she mentioned the villages of Hornbl*aw*ton – again her pronunciation was quite precise – and Stone Chapel, both of which were correct for her time, although the former is now called Hornbl*o*tton while the latter no longer exists.

Ramster also managed to unearth a manuscript from this period that recorded all the landed gentry in Somerset, and he was delighted to find the Lethbridges, James Stuart Mackenzie and Hugh Somerville all listed. Meanwhile Rose had also described how Mackenzie had hired the architect James Wyatt to renovate the stairs and banisters in the main house, and how a curse had been placed on the Mackenzies by Coinneach Odhar, the 'Brahan Seer'. And both these aspects of her story checked out too.

These signs were encouraging. Ramster was also satisfied there was no way Gwen was attempting to perpetrate some sort of elaborate fraud by having accessed similarly obscure manuscripts. So he was now ready to depart for England to conduct his own further research before Gwen and the others joined him.

In the library at Taunton he enquired about the word *tallet*, which Rose had used in connection with the roof of their cottage, and found that it meant a loft.

More impressive again was a discovery he made by pure luck. Rose had mentioned that a group of Quakers used to pass through her neighborhood to get to Alford, where they had a small 'meeting house'. When he looked into this further he discovered that, although in modern times there are meeting houses in virtually every town and in many villages, at that point they were rarer. But Alford was not listed in the main Quaker records from that time, and nor did anyone in Alford itself know of such meetings having taken place.

However, during his local research he and some assistants chanced upon a hoard of magazines from the period, and they happily flicked through them out of general interest and to get a feel for life in Somerset at that time. They did not expect to find a brief but clear reference to a meeting of Quakers in Alford. This was starting to be the sort of obscure information that even the most determined hoaxer was unlikely to have uncovered.

As if all this were not enough already, Gwen and the film crew then flew out to meet Ramster in London. After a little rest and acclimatization, Ramster again regressed Gwen to her life as Rose, and afterwards discussed the details consciously in the hope that her memories would now be closer to the surface as they tried to verify them.

This seemed to work because they then traveled to Somerset to meet Basil Cottle, an expert in local history from the University of Bristol who was to act as an independent witness throughout. She was given an unmarked map of Glastonbury and asked to point out any landmarks she recognized, and immediately identified Wearyall Hill, which lies to the southwest and which she had referred to back in Sydney. She also identified Tor Hill to the east, on which stands the famous ruined tower of St Michael's Church. She then pointed out the ruins of the abbey on the map, and for the first time described how two low pyramids had sat in the middle of the ruins, acting as a doorway. A local historian subsequently confirmed that this observation was correct according to medieval records.

Gwen's next stop was to be taken to the abbey itself, although blindfolded so as not to prejudice later attempts at navigation. When she first saw the ruins again she was clearly moved. The major difference, apart from the absence of the two pyramids, was apparently the way in which the site had been cleared of rubble and generally cleaned up for tourists – which in fact she found rather sterile and depressing.

But as she walked around the memories seemed to come flooding back. She lovingly caressed the carved feathers on the pillars of an arched doorway, exactly as she had described Rose doing all those years before. At this point she became quite understandably overwhelmed because, despite the detailed nature of her hypnotic recall, she had never been consciously certain of its validity. Until now when, just like Cynthia, she realized she really had stood in exactly this spot nearly two hundred years previously: 'The memory of this place brings the same old feelings and the feelings of peace. You wouldn't believe the feelings I get inside from seeing this place, you really wouldn't.'

The next task was for Gwen to attempt to find her former home, which the team felt sure had been in Hornblotton. She was blindfolded and taken to the outskirts of Ansford several miles to the east, which they also felt sure was the local village she had walked to once a week. Standing in a field she spotted a line of trees to the west that she thought were familiar, and the search was on.

She took them along a road for a short distance, but then stopped at a bend in the small village of Clanville. She said that in Rose's day there had been a row of five houses at this point, one of which sold cider. Now there were only two new houses and two old ones, one a mere ruin. But in the other the owner confirmed that his house had been built in 1742 and that a number of its contemporaries had only recently been knocked down. Not only that, but his family had a tradition that one of them had been a cider house – a point subsequently confirmed on an old map.

Gwen now left the road to the north and began to traverse the fields. It was not long before they came to the stream she had said would be there, but it was getting late so they decided to stop for the day. The next morning they returned and she led them along the stream, still heading west. In trance she had described how they would come to a fork, near which was a small waterfall, all of which they encountered after about a mile. In addition, although she had described some stepping stones near the fork that were no longer there, a local man was able to subsequently confirm they had been removed some forty years previously.

At the fork Gwen sensed she was close and sped off across a field, with the rest of the team struggling to keep up. After about half a mile her mood changed to one of trepidation as she stopped and stared at a building that could just be made out through the trees. When they reached it there were tiles on the roof rather than thatch, and it seemed to be just an old barn attached to a more modern home. But she insisted this was her old house.

Cottle asked Gwen to sketch the back of the house on the spot, and she came up with a rough drawing of a back window and door, and of a lean-to that she referred to as the drying room. When they walked around there was a lean-to, but only one window that looked as if it might have once been a door. Cottle was skeptical, yet Gwen was convinced this was her former home and, facing it again after an interval of several centuries, she broke down in tears for the first time.

Their differences were soon resolved. The team obtained permission to look inside, and the outline of an older window that was now bricked up lay exactly where she had said it would. Meanwhile there, in the roof, was a loft room or tallet.

This, surely, must be the end of Gwen's incredible story? No. There is one final, and even more amazing, twist. While in Sydney she had described how Rose had been at the abbey one day when she had cut her foot quite badly, and a local farmer called Brown had taken her to his cottage nearby to bandage it up. He was kind, but the forthright Rose was upset that he had been stealing flagstones from the abbey ruins to cover the floor of his home, because on this particular journey she was sharing the cart with one that had unusual markings on it. Ramster asked her to draw these while still in trance and she very roughly sketched a variety of curved lines and spirals.

Of course they had already had incredible success with Gwen, far more than they could possibly have hoped. But Ramster knew that the crowning glory would be if they could locate the farmer's cottage and the flagstone, even though the chances were probably slim at best.

So, on their final day together, they assembled at the abbey and Gwen headed off. On the way they passed the George and Pilgrim Inn, which she had described and accurately drawn for Ramster back in Sydney – with a long bow window on one side, an arch in the middle for coaches, and two triangular, pointed structures on the roof. The only difference was that she had called it 'The Pilgrim's Inn', which was correct for Rose's time.

They pressed on, heading west out of Glastonbury towards Meare. At one point they had to skirt an embankment where a new ring road was being constructed, and of course the majority of the buildings had changed too. Nevertheless she persevered, and they eventually came to a bridge over a stream. Now they needed to locate what Rose had described as the second in a row of five thatched cottages that lay nearby.

Gwen left the road and walked along the stream for a short while, before pointing to a dilapidated building on the other side that on closer inspection turned out to be a chicken shed. The farmer, Dennis Simmonds, confirmed that it had been a row of five thatched cottages, which had deteriorated so much that the end ones had been pulled down. What was left had a corrugated iron roof, while the windows were open holes, but it looked as though the basis of the original, second cottage was still there.

The next problem was that for decades the floor had been covered in droppings. Simmonds kindly agreed to clean it overnight, and was himself amazed to find dark blue flagstones that clearly matched others still remaining at the abbey. But what of the one with the markings? Gwen pointed to one that seemed to have faint patterns on it, and anticipation mounted as they washed it off and brushed it with talcum powder so that the markings stood out.

Although faint, there were some definite similarities with the ones Gwen had drawn. And even if one were to take the view that this was purely a coincidence given their relatively random nature, the mere fact that she knew there were flagstones from the abbey buried underneath all the detritus is surely impressive enough.

The main argument used by skeptics when discussing past-life regression is similar to that for children's past-life cases. They suggest that subjects are constructing narratives from normally acquired information that they themselves have forgotten they learned, which is formally called 'cryptomnesia'. In other words they rarely suggest deliberate fraud, but they do suggest delusion.

In this context another fascinating case study is provided by the 'Bloxham Tapes', which were the subject of a bestselling book and BBC television documentary in the 1970s. The star was a Welsh housewife dubbed 'Jane Evans', who recalled impressive historical details of a number of different lives. In the most striking she was the wife of a children's tutor in Roman Britain; a persecuted Jewess in twelfth-century York; and a maidservant to a wealthy financier in fifteenth-century France.

The investigators took great care to establish what the sources of normally acquired information might have been, and to show that most details Jane recalled for each life could only be found in various obscure reference works. However they overlooked one major source, and that was historically based fiction. Indeed skeptics were able to show that her Roman life was closely based on a historical novel, despite her use of strange accents and strong apparent emotions while in trance. So it's clear that we need to tread carefully.

Nevertheless it turns out that Jane's French life can't be explained in the same way, despite skeptics' claims. In fact it's arguably one of the strongest cases on record because, for example, she recalled the financier having been given a 'golden apple encrusted with jewels'. The existence of this piece was subsequently traced by a local historian to contemporary court records, written of course in medieval French, which hadn't been accessed for centuries. Such obscure information surely wouldn't appear in any work of fact or fiction, nor in any other normal source.

The same is, of course, true of the most obscure facts in Ramster's cases. But these remain so poorly recognized outside his native Australia that few skeptics have even heard of them.

Yet even if normal explanations fail in these strong cases, could the alternative paranormal explanations that we rejected for children's past lives apply this time round? Again some sort of universal memory seems unlikely to be able to account for the depth of emotion felt by Cynthia and Gwen when they were reunited with their former surroundings. And while on the face of it possession again appears to be a more feasible solution, neither woman showed any of the unusual behavioral traits normally associated with this. Again, therefore, the recall of individual past lives seems the most likely explanation for these two cases – and perhaps for many others as well.

We've spent some considerable time on the stories of James, Swarnlata, Cynthia and Gwen. But this is because our second key proposition, which stems from them, has significant and far-reaching implications:

souls have many lives, not just one

So far so good. But is there any evidence that can help us to really understand what happens after we die – that is in the time between lives? And does this evidence show a continuity across many lives that reinforces our conclusion concerning individual soul memories?

the hall of records

What follows is Gwen's account of what happened *after* Rose's death, again elicited by Ramster using hypnosis, although his questions are omitted here.

'I died in bed, and old [Dr] Andrews was sitting by my bed with my father and Bessie. Then my father, he walked out the door. And Bessie, she be crying [these seem to be the last remnants of Rose's Somerset brogue before her soul-self takes over].

'Then I saw a lady, I knew her last time [I died]. She was with a man in a long robe, and he put out his hand and I took it and I went with him. I began to feel very light, no weight, nothing to hold me down, everything was light, like floating but not floating. There was no pain, and I was very aware, so much more aware of feelings and senses, and thoughts, almost as if you didn't have to speak. It was like being made of air. Free, free, so free.

'Before I left I remember standing beside the bed and looking down at the body. I'd wasted away, and I felt free, so free. I was just standing there looking at myself and I wondered why Bessie was crying. Then I realized I was dead and the life was no more, and I couldn't go back, it was over. I could see Bessie crying. I knew she couldn't see me, nor could she hear me. I would have liked to talk to her, but I was dead and could remain there no more.

'I was taken to a place and was told to rest, which I did. I don't really know for how long, but I was being pulled back because Bessie was feeling so sad missing me, and it was holding me back. I came down to see her again and I tried to tell her to let me go, not to hold me back, because it hurts. After a time she finally did.

'I was taken to a place where I met a man who looked like an Egyptian. From the place where I was told to rest we walked along a grassy path. Everywhere was grass and there was water. It was in many ways similar to earth, but you could put your feet into the water and take them out again without having to dry them, as they didn't get wet! He said it was because we were in spirit.

'We walked to the Hall of Records and that was where I met the Egyptian. He was so kind, he showed me all I had done, and things I should have done but didn't do. The place was like a library and it's full of records. It was a big place, a very big place. It had a long corridor with a sort of gold light everywhere inside. He showed me my life, but I could see it in my mind, not on paper, all the things I'd done, things I needed to do and didn't do.

'The thing I needed to do was to be more conscious of other people. I was selfish, I only thought about myself and where I lived, my home, and not the poor people in the village and the poor children. I should have helped, but I didn't. His voice is almost music, and there is a light that shines around him. When he looks at you his eyes seem to read what you are thinking, he seems to know.

'I was told that in the Hall of Records there is a file on every living soul that ever incarnated, and each time we have to see what fools we've been, what mistakes we've made. We have two paths to choose. If you take the wrong path it's all against you. If you take the right path it's all for you, and it's balanced out in the Hall of Records. It's all there, every page, almost every thought and every deed is there, every book, every spoken word you can find. It's gold inside, lit up with a gold light, pure light. Everything in there is knowledge, and the keeper, the Egyptian in this plane, looks after and controls the records.

'We can't touch the higher levels. We can go to the lower levels to try and help, but we can't touch the higher levels until we've been lifted up there as our right. He can go to the higher levels. He can come and go as he pleases, he is close to the master, but you know he's there. You can feel he [the master] is there, but I don't think he's like we are, I think he's different somehow. I don't think he's like us, I think he's pure spirit. It's just a feeling you have that he's so far out of your reach. You wish you could touch him, but you can't, he is far above us.

'We reincarnate to learn, to learn knowledge, understanding and compassion. Those who do not learn must come again and again and again... That is why we must come back, until our souls are pure enough to stay up there on that level. Because our thoughts are what makes us, and what colors our soul.

'When we leave the Hall of Records the Egyptian bows, puts his hands together and smiles. When the door shuts, you know what you have to do, it's all in your mind without him saying a lot. It's in your mind, it's there.

'After going over my life we left the library and were back on the grass. We paddled in the water and, as I said, didn't need to dry ourselves. There were boats on the water, all green grass and trees greener than anywhere. The flowers were all alive, no dead flowers. Around the lake on the other side there were more trees, flowers, and birds, pretty birds, and oh, such beautiful music! We sat and talked under the trees and rested. It was a beautiful place. The only time I became worried was when someone thought of me and I was pulled back, and it's sad.

'Finally a man came, he said I must go back to earth. I didn't want to go back but I had to. He said there were people who needed me and I must help. There were two families who needed me, and I had to choose. I could do what I had to do with both families, but I had to choose, and I must go back. I rested on that plane until it became time to go back to earth.'

Ramster wasn't the only therapist to be amazed when he discovered that some of his subjects could recall lucid details, not only of their past lives, but of their time between lives as well. A number of other 'interlife' pioneers in America and Canada made the same discovery in the mid-1970s. All of a sudden ordinary people like Gwen were delivering profound insights into what happens in what we might refer to as the 'light realms'.

But, unlike past-life recall, this isn't the sort of experience that can be verified. So can it really be regarded as at all reliable? The reason we might answer 'yes' is that these pioneers were all operating independently in what were pre-internet days, and yet the reports from their hundreds of subjects were broadly consistent. These people had no particular religious or spiritual background, but instead came from a broad cross section of Western society. And not only were the books the original pioneers published not widely enough read to have had a significant influence, but most of them had completed their early research before their books even came out.

Before we get carried away we should appreciate that interlife experiences are extremely fluid, which is why it's probably a mistake to attempt to over-categorize them. For example, Gwen talks a great deal about a semi-physical place with grass, trees, flowers and water, and even of a 'Hall of Records' run by someone she calls the 'Egyptian'. Some other subjects have reported seeing similar things, and have even referred to a 'hall' or 'library'. But others tend to perceive both their environment, and any other souls they meet, in more energetic and less physical form. It seems that much of what we experience, at least while we're getting used to being in the light again, depends on the assumptions we bring with us from our earthly lives. Our general level of soul experience may also be relevant.

Nevertheless, despite this fluidity, we can broadly identify five main elements of the interlife experience that are consistent across all the pioneering research. And Gwen's account provides a fine example because she at least touches on most of them.

So what are these elements? And, more to the point, what can they tell us that might help us to better understand how to approach our everyday lives?

1 Transition and Healing

Gwen talks about being met by a man and a woman who are there to guide her after death. And most interlife subjects talk about being met by deceased friends or family, or other spirits of light who help them to make the transition. The same is also true of most near-death subjects, as we saw earlier with Pam.

Gwen also talks about feeling 'light, very aware and free' as she's released from her body, and again most interlife and near-death subjects talk in similar terms. It seems that we have to shed the denser emotions and energies associated with the physical world so that our soul energy gradually becomes lighter. We might refer to this as 'delayering', and it seems that this raising of vibrations is essential to allow us to re-enter the higher frequencies of the light realms.

This process also seems to be closely tied into emotional healing, although the extent that this is required depends on the degree of trauma suffered in the previous life – and death. Gwen seems to need little after her life as Rose, because she's merely told to rest. But other subjects describe incredible 'cleansing showers of energy' that invigorate and lighten them, and wash away many of the stresses and strains of the physical world.

But not all is sweetness and light. The evidence suggests that some souls who are heavily traumatized don't even realize or accept that they're dead. As 'ghosts' they remain tightly focused on and attached to the physical, unable to let go of their deep emotions of fear, anger, jealousy, hatred or revenge, and often feeling they have unfinished business.

It seems that the energy of such spirits is so dense that they remain unaware of, or at least unable to move into, the light. Instead they hang around in what we might refer to as the 'intermediate plane', the nearest to the physical in terms of density of vibrations. And any 'astral travelers' who encounter this realm, whether via projection or meditation or drugs, rightly report that it's extremely unpleasant. Indeed, if there is any such place as 'hell', this is it. But it appears that these spirits are certainly not condemned to live in such torment for eternity.

2 Past-Life Review

We've all heard how our life flashes in front of us when we think we're going to die. And the idea of reviewing the life just lived is again common to not only interlife but also near-death experiences, as we saw earlier with George. It seems that sometimes we have help with this from two possible sources. On the one hand 'spirit guides' – that is, experienced souls who are always on hand to help us. And on the other various 'elders' – even wiser souls who help us to plot a path through our successions of lives.

Like Gwen, subjects often describe these reviews as taking place in a library-type environment, although the books often seem to 'come alive' like a film. Others suggest that they can 'enter' the film to replay various events, or even to role-play them by doing things differently and seeing what happens. And some even report that they can place themselves in the shoes of others, to see exactly what effect their own actions had – which, intriguingly, seems to tie in with the effect of the natural hallucinogen iboga.

Above all, and unlike in most religions, interlife research suggests that the only judgment in this review process comes, if at all, from ourselves. This is because our 'soul perspective' is totally unlike our human outlook, and cannot include self-deception or excuses. All our actions and, even more important, intentions are laid bare – and these are all that matter because, as Gwen says, they're 'what makes us, and what colors our soul'. Some souls find this dramatic change of perspective extremely uncomfortable, of course. So more often than not our spirit guides and elders are there to calm and reassure us, rather than to judge.

3 Soul Group Interaction

Interlife research suggests that all of us have a 'group' of 'soul mates' with whom we work closely over many lives. But the relationships can vary. Sometimes we're lovers, sometimes siblings, sometimes parents or children, sometimes close friends – and sometimes even enemies, just to spice things up. We can also change sex from one life to the next, which is perhaps a better explanation of why some people carry over gender identity issues than the simplistic 'nature versus nurture' debate.

When we reunite with our soul mates on our return to the light it's always a profoundly moving experience. We finally feel like we're 'really home'. Gwen doesn't recall meeting up with her soul group in that particular session, but she does insist that 'we reincarnate to learn'. And the evidence suggests that the primary aim of all souls is to gather experience in order to learn and grow. So our time with our soul group often involves discussions about lives we've shared, how we reacted to each other, what we handled well and what we could have handled better. And it appears that the ability to replay and role-play events is extremely useful for this learning process.

But what do we really mean by 'learning'? And how does this relate to traditional ideas of 'karma'?

the guilt that wouldn't go

Jenny Saunders first visited the pioneering interlife psychiatrist Joel Whitton at the University of Toronto because of sexual problems. He was known locally as the 'lost cause doctor' because he could cure people when all other therapies had failed.

Over a prolonged and difficult period of conventional regression he managed to establish that she had been cruelly abused by her mother as a child. She therefore avoided sex because any feelings of pleasure brought on by sexual stimulation were immediately replaced by emotional pain and intense anger. This realization should at least have started the healing process, but Jenny's symptoms persisted.

Whitton had also discovered that she was terrified of having a child of her own, and not long before becoming his patient had had an abortion after a rare sexual encounter. Apart from the obvious fact that she might not want to repeat the mistakes of her own mother, he could find nothing else in her current life to explain this fear. So he decided to extend the regression back beyond her childhood, at which point the following two lives unfolded.

As Lucy Bowden she had been the poverty-stricken single mother of a mentally retarded child in London in the late seventeenth century. In those days everyone regarded such children as a mere burden to be disposed of, but Lucy cherished and protected her child with all her might. She rarely left her rented attic room because of her fear that someone, whether well meaning or not, might try to rid her of her 'burden'.

But one day she went to fetch some provisions, and stopped to have a drink with some friends at an inn. Not used to alcohol, time slipped by quickly until she realized she had been gone for some hours, and rushed home. But when she turned the corner into her street her blazing house was surrounded by curious onlookers. Pushing through the crowd, she realized there was nothing she could do to save her child – and her unbearable inner torment was to set up a recurring pattern.

In another life in the mid-nineteenth century Jenny was Angela, a young girl abandoned by her parents and brought up in a Chicago orphanage. At sixteen she left the harsh institution behind to seek a new life in the mid-west, ending up as a barmaid and part-time prostitute in a small town in Colorado. The local doctor fell in love with her and she became pregnant by him.

But, unbeknown to her, the local parson began berating the doctor that his child would be born out of wedlock to a woman of ill repute. Eventually he blackmailed the doctor into agreeing that it should be committed to an institution to preserve its moral sanctity.

So as soon as the child was born the parson, the doctor and two assistants came to collect the baby, wrestling it from the convalescing Angela's startled grasp. Instinctively she reached for a shotgun she always kept under her bed for protection, but in the ensuing struggle the weapon discharged right at the baby and the assistant carrying it, killing both instantly.

Again Angela's shock and remorse was unbearable, but worse was to come. Their curiosity piqued by the sound of a gunshot, and with the parson egging them on to punish the 'murderer', six cowboys entered the room and dragged her off to a cattle shed, from which she never emerged.

After reliving these horrors Jenny wept uncontrollably in Whitton's office – maybe for the first time in her life.

How should we interpret Jenny's experiences? The traditional view of karma, still expressed in many spiritual circles, is that it involves some sort of 'law of action and reaction'. So, if we have problems in our current life, this is often assumed to be a reaction to something we did wrong in a previous one.

But how can this apply in Jenny's case? She was primarily an innocent victim in not only her two past lives when she lost her child each time, but also in her current one in which she was abused as a child. This is clearly a 'repetitive' pattern of sorts, but not one in which she alternated between victim and perpetrator in a cycle of action and reaction.

Many people would nevertheless assume that she must have done something awful in other lives – ones that she didn't recall during her time with Whitton – to deserve such 'punishments'. But then we find that when Whitton regressed Jenny into the interlife, she perceived herself appearing before her elders in chains.

His interpretation was that, just as we've already seen with past-life reviews, she was meting out her own punishment because of her failure to forgive herself for letting her children down in her former lives. So she gave herself another difficult life, although with a rather different pattern, because that was what she felt she deserved.

It therefore seems that any repetitive patterns we set up from life to life will probably be quite complex, as in Jenny's case. And simplistic interpretations, especially if they involve suggestions of action and reaction, are unlikely to be of much use. What we do know is that with Whitton's help Jenny came to realize that she had to forgive herself for her past-life mistakes. And happily, when she left his office for the last time, she was no longer afraid. Indeed she was determined to have a child in this life too.

So it seems that the traditional idea of a karmic law of action and reaction, which determines our fate or even punishment from one life to the next, is entirely unhelpful and misleading.

But what about Gwen's insistence that we reincarnate to learn? We find that this sentiment is echoed time and again by interlife subjects. Indeed it's the most constant theme of all.

Regression evidence suggests that in the first instance all souls have to work on what we might refer to as 'emotional lessons'. That is we need to learn how to shift progressively away from fear-based emotions and attitudes such as impatience, guilt, shame, selfishness, humiliation, jealousy, anger, hatred and revenge towards more love-based ones such as patience, altruism, openness, understanding, forgiveness and acceptance. And in order to experience and understand them properly we need not only to feel them ourselves, but also to feel what it's like to have them directed at us by others.

So, even if they can be quite complex, it appears that we do tend to indulge in repetitive patterns of behavior as we attempt to master our emotions, either within one life or from one life to the next. But it's clear that this shouldn't be regarded as in any sense backward or abnormal. And one of our aims in all of this is to learn to moderate our emotional responses, not only to difficult but also favorable circumstances. Wise advice down the ages, from all over the world, has always been that we shouldn't get too carried away by our successes, nor become crushed by our failures.

What, then, do we make of difficult circumstances, such as severe disability, or emotional and financial deprivation? Clearly traditional views of these as karmic punishments for past misdeeds are totally misplaced. And even though there can of course be repetitive elements to them, modern evidence suggests that such circumstances are most often chosen by relatively experienced souls who want to speed up their growth. This indicates what we might refer to as a more 'progressive' pattern of behavior.

It also seems that more experienced souls increasingly choose to take on more 'altruistic lives', which tend to be primarily for other people's benefit and growth rather than their own. This can involve severe disability, but the most obvious example of a purely altruistic life is when a soul volunteers for a short life that'll end in childhood, or even before birth. Although such lives can sometimes be traumatic for the infants themselves, they tend to be far more aimed at challenging parents and other close relatives to learn to cope with the myriad emotions that surround such a tragic loss. And Jenny's two past lives involving young children are, of course, prime examples of this.

We're now in a position to make three more key propositions:

our many lives are not linked by a karmic law of action and reaction

we reincarnate to gather experience so we can grow

the only judgment after death comes from ourselves

4 Next-Life Planning

To continue with the next element of the interlife, while the idea of a past-life review may not be particularly novel, there is nothing in traditional religions to prepare us for the idea that we're involved in planning our own lives. Yet this is what the interlife evidence consistently suggests, and it has huge implications for the way we see ourselves.

But first let's look at the mechanics of this planning process. It seems that at the very least it'll involve an awareness of what sex we'll be, who our parents will be, where they live and what their circumstances are. However many subjects seem to receive a rather fuller preview, often describing it as akin to seeing a film that they can stop, rewind, fast-forward and even enter to fully experience what's going on. We may even be given a preview of several different lives, and be asked to choose which one we think will provide the best environment for our growth.

In Gwen's example she was at least told there were two families who needed her to help them in her next life after Rose – suggesting perhaps a more altruistic flavor – and that she could do what she had to do with either. So presumably she was given some sort of preview of each to allow her to make her choice, although this wasn't discussed in that session.

As usual, our spirit guides and elders are on hand to help with this planning process. We may also spend some time discussing our plans with other members of our soul group who'll be involved in that life, and even agreeing 'triggers' that'll help us to recognize them when we meet.

So what are the implications? If we can see detailed previews of our life, does this mean it's all totally predetermined? Apparently not. It seems that these glimpses merely represent the most probable outcome if we stick to our 'life plan'. The key point is that we still have complete free will to stray from this once in the physical world, because a predetermined experience would provide no opportunity for making decisions for ourselves – which is a major contributor to our growth. This also means that when we face difficult circumstances we would do well to accept responsibility for them. Not only did we choose them, but we did so to allow ourselves to grow. And we won't achieve this by attempting to put the blame on other people, a fickle God, or blind chance.

We can summarize this into two further key propositions:

we are responsible for all aspects of our lives because we plan and choose them

we always have free will to deviate from our life plan

5 Returning

Gwen seems to suggest that she was forced to return to the physical world. However the broader evidence suggests that most of us 'know' when it's time to continue gathering experiences in the physical, even if we may have some initial reluctance to leave our true home in the light.

Recent interlife research also suggests that when we return to the *physical we leave some soul energy behind to carry on with various activities in the light realms. But we take with us specific emotions we want to continue working with, and even past-life strengths that we may need to help us through difficult patches. It seems that this is achieved by what we might refer to as a 'relayering' process, in which we take on these heavier emotions as if putting on various layers of clothing.*

Our soul energy can begin to merge with the unborn child in the womb at any time from conception to birth. This is a gradual and sometimes difficult process, which seems to involve some sort of matching of the individual pattern and frequency of our soul energy to that of the developing brain. But we can also relax by floating out of the body for short periods, not only up until birth but even for some time afterwards.

Of course we all know how much babies sleep, and it seems that this is our way of becoming gradually accustomed to the physical again. In fact babies probably retain a significant memory of their true soul identity and connection to the light realms – which is why they should never be underestimated. However over time this connection gradually fades, for two main reasons. First, if it didn't we'd be constantly pining for the bliss of our true home. And second, if we remembered all about our life plan it would be like taking an exam with all the answers to hand – and we'd learn nothing.

And so begins another cycle on our lengthy round of gathering experience in the physical world. But how long does this reincarnation cycle go on for? And what happens when it's over?

All the evidence suggests that, broadly speaking, we keep coming back for as long as the physical world can offer us new experiences that'll allow us to grow. After that we can still come back sometimes to help others, or we can move on to other less physical planes to continue the process. Either way it seems that, in terms of the soul's overall journey, finishing with the 'earthly round' is only the end of the beginning.

But what of 'God'? Does He, She or It exist? Gwen's reference to 'the master' as an apparently separate being probably reflects a certain simplicity, because the answer is most likely 'yes, but not in the way you might think'. The central element of all mystical and transcendental experiences seems to be a brief glimpse of the 'Oneness' and interconnectedness of everything in the universe. This comes from experienced meditators, and from those who experiment with 'altered states' using hallucinogenic drugs. Most tellingly it's now also backed up by modern science.

So it seems that everything in the universe, both seen and unseen, is part of one interconnected whole or 'Unity' – often referred to simply as

'Source'. Indeed we might go as far as to propose that 'we're all One and all God'.

Because of this, some people suggest that the idea of us being individual souls is just an illusion. But in this book we've painstakingly amassed a great deal of evidence to the contrary. So is there a way of accepting both sides of the evidence – that is, for soul individuality and unity?

The answer is yes. What if soul consciousness is holographic? This would allow for us being individual aspects of Source, and full holographic representations of it, all at the same time. Remember that the principle of the hologram is that the part contains the whole, and yet is clearly distinguishable from it.

Let's conclude by daring to consider the biggest question of all: why does any of this happen in the first place? Some might think this is far beyond mere mortals and that we should leave well alone. But surely we should at least hazard a guess?

Some people suggest that we only need to recognize that we're part of the One to escape from the illusion of the reincarnation cycle. Yet what would be the point of the whole exercise if that was the case? Others maintain that the whole idea of soul individuality is an illusion, and that when we die our soul energy automatically reunites with Source. Meanwhile the new breed of spiritually oriented, theoretical scientists – or 'quantum mystics' – sometimes seem to struggle to put their theories about unity, interconnectedness, even multiple worlds and so on into a sensible, understandable, overall framework.

But what if the answer is actually dead simple? What if Source's primary aim, in diversifying into all the billions of holographic aspects of itself that operate in the various realms throughout the universe, is to experience all that is and can be? And what if, as individualized aspects of Source who have chosen to reincarnate on this planet, we are merely fulfilling a small part of that objective by gathering a balance of all the experiences available here?

So here are our three, final, key propositions:

we are all One and all God

soul consciousness is holographic, and represents the part and the whole all at the same time

the aim of Source is to experience all that is and can be

a personal story

It might be useful to conclude by saying a few words about my own story. If this little book is successfully finding its way to the type of person I hope will find it most stimulating and rewarding, we should share at least some things in common.

I was born in 1959, and brought up on the south coast of England. In common with so many households of my generation ours was at least nominally Christian, although I can't remember religion ever being discussed much. But we had to sit through lessons and sermons at school, and as soon as I started to really think for myself I realized that these left me cold. Without wishing to cause offence, from a purely theoretical perspective Christianity seemed to me to be completely irrational.

So it was that I became convinced that religion was for those who *needed* to believe because they were too feeble to exist without that vital crutch. By contrast, I decided, real power and strength comes from within oneself, not from some external deity. What I didn't know then in my youthful arrogance, and what prominent atheists like Richard Dawkins have still not understood, is that there is far more to this than meets the eye.

After I left school I led a rather uneventful life for a while. Instead of traveling the world in my gap year like my more adventurous friends, I worked for a merchant bank in the City. Then off to UCL to study Economics, badly, before following all the sensible advice and going into accountancy.

This was a great training in many ways, but it wasn't really for me. So, after qualifying, a major career change saw me join the yuppies selling computer software. This was the selfish, money-obsessed 1980s, and I fitted right in. In fact I had been racing bikes for some time, with limited success, but the injuries were piling up and I turned to racing cars. With my loud suits and ties, mullet haircut, racing Porsche and blonde on my arm, I surely was the man. Or so I thought. Spirituality? Pah!

So what happened between then and now? Nothing sudden. Just a gradual intensification of a gut feeling that there was something more – coupled with various coincidences, perhaps better termed synchronicities, that led me away from that world and into this. By the mid-1990s, although I was now working in consultancy rather than sales, I was becoming increasingly sick of the world of commerce. The preoccupation with money and contracts and deals and deadlines and targets and progress and success and...

So one day I just quit.

Admittedly I had a bit of money put away although – surprise, surprise – it turned out to be nowhere near enough. My decision was also made far easier by having no family to support. So what was I going to do?

All I knew was that I had a vague desire to start researching some of the ancient mysteries that a partner had recently introduced me to. And so it began. Having had conspicuously little academic success – at least not in any truly creative, intellectual sense – I had no idea that I'd end up writing. I especially had no idea that that writing would eventually take a spiritual course. But it has. And in particular I've found myself drawn towards developing the kind of evidence-based spirituality that you've read about here.

But if I'm honest this recent leg of my journey has been a real struggle. Not just financially at times, but even more emotionally. Constantly trying to compete with hundreds of other spiritual books, let alone those about cookery and football and celebrities and so on, just to get what you hope is a useful idea in front of people. Trying to maintain integrity in your work when others want you to 'sex it up' or cut it down or generally mangle it to make it more commercial. Constantly being promised support, and that one breakthrough you need, only to have your hopes dashed at the last minute.

But of course I must remember to practice what I preach! So I recognize that all this has helped me personally to grow, and to learn some really important lessons about arrogance, expectations, impatience, blockages and positive thinking. More than this, though, there's one major reason why I've persevered even when I felt completely crushed. It's because I believe the concept of 'Rational Spirituality' – which I've been developing for a number of years now, and which is what this book is all about – is sufficiently powerful and unique that it can really make a difference at a crucial point in our collective learning curve.

Why? For thousands of years we've had morality-based religions of all shapes and sizes, sometimes giving hope and succor, but just as often bringing domination, suppression and even annihilation. Then along came science, and it started to prove that our religions were not quite all they'd been cracked up to be. So the smart intellectual money began to shift entirely in a scientific and materialist direction.

Now at last, thanks to the work of many different pioneers from many fields, we can see the real possibility of bringing science and spirituality back together, as they once were in Classical times. But the full power of *all* the modern research at our disposal should be harnessed – that is the evidence that points not only towards universal but also individual soul consciousness. Hopefully the concept of the holographic soul may have a part to play in this – but only in as much as it modernizes what the most profound spiritual sources from across the ages have always tried to tell us.

Rational Spirituality has its roots firmly planted in the fertile soil of modern evidence and logic. By contrast traditional religions tend to be based on unquestioning reliance on ancient scripture, and modern interpretations of it. The motto 'evidence not faith' is intended to convey this fundamental difference in approach. But that's not to say that faith, or perhaps better trust, doesn't have its place. Total trust in our ability to face and pass the tests we set for ourselves and to consciously create our own reality – with assistance from our higher selves, spirit guides and the universe in general if we're open to it – is fundamental to a Rational Spiritual worldview. Nor does it underestimate the power and majesty of transformative spiritual experiences, or underplay the ultimate spiritual message of universal, unconditional love.

Perhaps most important of all, in contrast to many traditional religions, Rational Spirituality doesn't attempt to provide a definitive moral code. Instead it merely encourages us to take personal responsibility for applying its framework of understanding to our own lives.

It is, surely, an idea whose time has come.

source references

Anyone interested in examining the evidence in this book in more detail, including further cases, more in depth analysis and full source references, can find all this in *The Big Book of the Soul*.

Meanwhile a simple, short companion volume, *Your Holographic Soul – and how to make it work for you*, provides more details on this concept in particular, as well as self-help advice based on the framework of Rational Spirituality.

THE CRYING BABY

Phyllis Atwater, *Beyond The Light* (Thorsons, 1995), chapter 1, pp. 16-17 and chapter 5, pp. 78-82 (for further analysis concerning the baby girl's broken hip see www.ianlawton.com/nde4.htm).

Phillip Berman, *The Journey Home* (Pocket Books, 1998), chapter 2, pp. 31-7 (reproduced at www.ianlawton.com/nde3.htm).

HOTEL CALIFORNIA

Dr Michael Sabom, *Light and Death* (Zondervan, 1998), chapter 3 and chapter 10, pp. 184-9.

THE GI JOE DOLLS

Wes Milligan, 'The Past Life Memories of James Leininger', *Acadiana Profile Magazine*, December 2004 (reproduced at www.ianlawton.com/cpl3.htm).

Leininger, Bruce and Andrea, *Soul Survivor*, Grand Central Publishing, 2009.

THE 1200 RUPEES

Dr Ian Stevenson, Twenty Cases Suggestive of Reincarnation (University Press of Virginia, 1974), chapter II, pp. 67-91.

THE CHATEAU, BURIED FLAGSTONE AND HALL OF RECORDS

Dr Peter Ramster, *The Search for Lives Past* (Somerset Film & Publishing, 1990), chapter 6, pp. 211-43, chapters 2-3, and chapter 2, pp. 57-61.

See also 'The Reincarnation Experiments' documentary produced by Ramster in 1983 (available via www.ianlawton.com/rsvideos.htm).

THE GUILT THAT WOULDN'T GO

Dr Joel Whitton and Joe Fisher, *Life Between Life* (Warner Books, 1988), chapter 12.

further reading

This is a selection of the most important introductory books on each topic, which are mostly by professional psychiatrists and psychologists.

GENERAL

Lawton, Ian, *The Big Book of the Soul* (Rational Spirituality Press, 2008) and *Your Holographic Soul* (Rational Spirituality Press, 2010).

NEAR-DEATH EXPERIENCES

Dr Peter Fenwick, *The Truth in the Light* (Berkley Books, 1997).

Dr Raymond Moody, *Life After Life* (Bantam, 1976).

Dr Kenneth Ring, *Life At Death* (Quill, 1982).

CHILDREN'S PAST-LIFE MEMORIES

Carol Bowman, *Children's Past Lives* (Bantam, 1997).

Dr Ian Stevenson, *Twenty Cases Suggestive of Reincarnation* (University Press of Virginia, 1974) and *Children Who Remember Previous Lives* (University Press of Virginia, 1987).

Dr Jim Tucker, *Life Before Life* (Piatkus, 2006).

PAST-LIFE REGRESSION

Dr Edith Fiore, *You Have Been Here Before* (Ballantine Books, 1979).

Dr Peter Ramster, *The Truth about Reincarnation* (Rigby, 1980) and *The Search for Lives Past* (Somerset Film & Publishing, 1990).

Dr Hans TenDam, *Exploring Reincarnation* (Rider, 2003).

Andy Tomlinson, *Healing the Eternal Soul* (O Books, 2006).

Dr Helen Wambach, *Reliving Past Lives* (Hutchinson, 1979).

Dr Roger Woolger, *Other Lives, Other Selves* (Bantam, 1988).

INTERLIFE REGRESSION

Dolores Cannon, *Between Death and Life* (Ozark, 1993).

Dr Shakuntala Modi, *Remarkable Healings* (Hampton Roads, 1997).

Dr Michael Newton, *Journey of Souls* (Llewellyn, 1994) and *Destiny of Souls* (Llewellyn, 2000).

Andy Tomlinson, *Exploring the Eternal Soul* (O Books, 2007).

Dr Helen Wambach, *Life Before Life* (Bantam, 1979).

Dr Joel Whitton, *Life Between Life* (Warner Books, 1988).

Note also that there are brief references to the interlife in both Fiore's and Ramster's books listed in the past-life section.

your holographic soul
and how to make it work for you

ian lawton

questions

is there more to life than just the material world?	5
do we possess a soul that survives our death?	7
who or what is God?	9
are we all One, and is everything just an illusion?	11
in what way are our souls holographic?	14
why is the universe here at all?	16
do we have many lives?	19

suggestions

forget karma, experience is all that matters	22
strive to be motivated by love, not fear	27
take personal responsibility for everything	30
search for the contentment within	33
love yourself first	35
meditate regularly and develop your intuition	38
drop the mask and face up to your lower self	42
consciously create the future you desire	45
actively surrender to the universe	49
use your soul rather than human perspective	51

This book would be a mere shadow of itself were it not for the outstanding contributions of a number of very dear friends. It wasn't planned that way. I got myself in the zone and penned the first version in a week. I had approached various people to have a read of the manuscript, but I confidently assumed they'd all tell me how wonderful it was and just suggest a few minor changes. I was wrong.

With this being a major departure from my normal, somewhat academic writing style, the main feedback was that I was tending to lecture the reader rather than guiding them along with me. Luckily my bruised ego did not stop me from seeing the constructiveness of this feedback, and so began a process that was clearly mapped out by all of us, and by the universe, long ago.

It also became clear that every one of us had a particular skill or outlook to bring to the party. I'm sure I sorely tried everyone's patience, sending out version after version for feedback, but to their eternal credit they stuck with the process over several months. The wonderful thing was that each new set of suggestions was so obviously going to strengthen the book, so much so that rather than seeing them as a threat and yet more work, I learned to welcome them. I think we can all say now that we're genuinely proud of this book, and of the process by which it came about. But I can't emphasize enough how much it's truly a collaborative effort.

To be more specific, my heartfelt thanks and love go out to Judy Hall and Hans TenDam for their generous cover quotes. To Tim Byford for his breadth and depth of knowledge of comparative religion. To Andy Tomlinson and Toni Winninger, whose inputs included feedback from their respective channels. To Hazel Newton, Janet Treloar, Peter Jenkins and Sue Liburd for going beyond the call of duty in the time and effort they put in on multiple versions. To Sue Stone and Pam Rosling, who rightly suggested that I needed to simplify and explain especially the early parts of the book to give it a far broader audience and appeal. To Ken Huggins, who put in huge efforts as final editor, a position thrust upon him in a rather de facto manner because of his evident thoroughness and pursuit of clarity. And to Stephen Gawtry. Not only did he come up with the subtitle in an instant, but he altered my perspective of both the interplay between experience and illusion, and also of active surrender. Without these significant shifts the book would be much the poorer. He was also the one who quite rightly questioned whether I'd be able to fit everyone's name on the spine ;-)

In addition I owe a great deal to Hazel and Sue S for another reason. In the last six months they've made sure that at last I understood how to put positive living into practice on a consistent basis, instead of just understanding the theory and applying it sporadically.

Meanwhile I couldn't have approached this book with such enthusiasm and freshness without the prescient advice of my great pal Neil Trevethan. After many years of concentration on writing and research, and of frustration as my attempts to be heard seemed to fall on deaf ears, he insisted that I take a break for most of last year.

How right he was. I took time out to collect driftwood with which to make mirrors and other artwork. To completely rebuild a classic sports motorcycle, after years of not getting my hands dirty. And to trek the length and breadth of the fantastic scenery of the Isle of Purbeck, which I'm now lucky enough to call my home. That's why, when I talk about that pure joy of life that comes from just being in nature and from finding inner peace and contentment, I'm at last talking not theoretically but from experience.

Last, but by no means least, I am deeply thankful to the various guides and other beings of light who pushed and prodded us as we struggled to get the balance of this book right. I hope we stayed open enough to hear you properly.

Ian Lawton
February 2010

Do you need to know anything about spirituality to make sense of this book?

No. Every effort has been made to keep it as clear and simple as possible, but everyone's different. So if you feel yourself getting a little lost please persevere. This book contains important insights and all will become clear.

What can you expect to get out of reading it?

The aim is to cover pretty much all of the main strands of spiritual theory and practice, and to introduce the concept of the holographic soul. So in the first part of the book we'll use the answers to a series of key *questions* to establish a sensible, modern, rational framework of spirituality that you can use to make sense of your existence.

    Then in the second part we'll turn to various *suggestions* as to how this framework might influence your practical approach to life.

questions

Anyone interested in the full details of the evidence referred to in this first part, along with source references, can find them in *The Big Book of the Soul*.

Meanwhile for a shorter and simpler version that includes a selection of important near-death-experience and reincarnation cases, see *The Little Book of the Soul*.

is there more to life than just the material world?

While most people reading this book will surely answer 'yes' to this question, some opening observations to back this up will be useful.

First, unlike traditional religious approaches, much of the material presented in summary in this part of the book isn't based on mere belief at all. Instead it's underpinned by a wide variety of evidence, and so comes under the heading of what we might refer to as 'Rational Spirituality'. Its motto is *evidence not faith*.

So to have a spiritual worldview, although not necessarily a religious one, does *not* make us fools who are too weak to face up to the grim prospect of extinction after death. Instead it actually means we're adopting the most logical response to the mounting evidence now on the table from a variety of fields of research.

Despite this, leading atheist intellectuals have recently been mounting an increasingly determined attack on those who have any sort of spiritual or religious leanings. They despair at the havoc still wrought around the world in the name of traditional religions that, being faith-based, can easily be written off as irrational. This is perhaps understandable. That they then throw the spiritual baby out with the bathwater is less so.

The basic debate between atheists and believers has long centered on the issue of evolution versus creation. And atheist criticisms of hardline creationism rightly reflect its failure to deal with a wealth of archaeological, geological and biological evidence in support of evolution. But here's the crucial question:

Does evolution occur by chance, or does some sort of deliberate design process lie behind it?

In respect of the *ongoing* evolution of the many and varied life forms on planet earth, can all the steps in the chain be explained by natural selection and so on? Or do we need to postulate that some unseen force sometimes gives the process a nudge? This is an incredibly complex debate that may never be conclusively proved one way or the other.

But there's one particular piece of evidence that's often overlooked, even though arguably it provides the coup de grace for a spiritual worldview. It involves the concept of evolution, but not just of life on planet earth. Instead it deals with the very existence of the physical universe as a whole, and what happened at the *outset*.

In short, it seems there are about three dozen 'universal, fundamental constants' that govern the observable universe. These include the speed of light for example, and they are so highly specific and 'finely tuned' that some commentators make a strong and hugely important claim... that if the value of any one of them was even slightly different, the conditions for the physical universe to exist at all would simply not have been met.

So did these universal constants arise by pure chance, or by deliberate design?

Those atheist scientists who accept this idea of a finely tuned universe insist that it simply means all possible universes exist with all possible values for what are in fact variables. They're then able to conclude that we just happen to be experiencing the one universe that struck it lucky with the right conditions for galaxies, solar systems, planets and life to evolve.

But this would imply that there are an infinite number of universes with no life at all. It's similar although not identical to the idea that there are multiple versions of this universe all playing out at the same time, in which our actions are only minutely differentiated. Do these ideas strike you as philosophically elegant?*

By contrast, consider the concept of a 'metaverse'. In simple terms we can think of this as the more fundamental universe that lies behind or beyond our universe. Now, what if this metaverse is an intelligent entity or life form with a consciousness of its own? And what if each time it creates a new universe it uses the knowledge gained previously to refine its creation? Many people find this a far more plausible explanation.

Seen in this light, the evolution-versus-design debate ceases to have any real meaning. The key issue is no longer design *or* evolution, but design *for* evolution.

Arguably this provides a key foundation stone for any sort of a rational, spiritual worldview.

---

* This term will be used at various key points. It's intended to convey a number of things, not all of which can easily be put into words, but chief among them is whether something strikes you as an intelligent yet simple solution to a question or problem.

do we possess a soul that survives our death?

You might be pleased to learn that this too isn't just wishful thinking, as skeptics would have you believe. There's plenty of evidence to suggest that our brain is merely the instrument that our soul consciousness uses to express itself in the physical world. It isn't the *source* of our thoughts or memories.

And these will continue to exist after we're dead, because of course it's only our physical body that perishes. Our consciousness will still be alive. Indeed the evidence suggests it'll be far more alive than it's ever been while confined in the limitations of our body.

What about heaven and hell? Do they exist?

All the evidence suggests that whatever we *expect* to happen when our soul leaves the body is pretty much what *will* happen. Many of you will already be aware that we create our own reality via our thoughts and intentions even in the physical world, something we'll discuss much more in the second part of the book. But we do so even more obviously and immediately in the nonphysical realms we encounter after death.

So if we think we'll see crystal castles on snow-capped mountain tops, that's what we'll get. If we think we'll see meadows festooned with wild flowers of all hues, that's what we'll get. Or if we think we'll see forests or beaches, or meet with our departed parents, grandparents, uncles, aunts, spouse or whoever, then *that's* what we'll get.

Will this last?

No. The evidence suggests that sooner or later we won't need all these imaginative creations to support us. We'll be able to see these other realms for what they really are. That is, myriad nonphysical 'planes of consciousness' each with a different 'frequency', to which we're attracted according to our soul's stage of growth and therefore 'energy vibration'. These are best thought of as different aspects[*] of what are collectively referred to as the 'light realms', or just 'the light'.

[*] Aspects rather than levels because the latter misleadingly suggest some sort of hierarchy.

What if we think we've been so bad that we'll be met by the devil? Does a fiery torment await?

It seems the same rules still apply, and again that's what we'll get. Or, in a slightly less extreme version, we'll find ourselves in what some have described as a 'grey place' laden with dark and dense emotions. But in either case we'll be judging and punishing *ourselves*. And the evidence suggests that at some point we'll realize enough is enough and move properly into the light, although sometimes only with a little help from human or spirit guides.

But what if we think there's nothing after death, and that our consciousness dies with our body?

Then it seems likely we'll be in for something of a shock, in as much as we'll find that *something* is still thinking thoughts. Other than that, guess what? The evidence suggests that initially we'll just see nothing. Zip. A void. But, sooner or later, our thoughts will conjure up *something*. And then we'll just be on the same path as everyone else, albeit perhaps with some initial confusion.

What if someone is still preoccupied with some unfinished business on the earth plane?

This might happen if, for example, they died suddenly, violently or early. Even then they might go into the light as normal. But if their emotions remain strong enough at the point of death they might seek to resolve them by refusing to break their ties with the physical world, thereby remaining in a sort of limbo plane. They might even attach their energy to living people with similar emotions, preoccupations or habits. But they too will eventually realize that it's time to leave and go into the light, albeit that again they might need some help.

who or what is God?

Even if you've been comfortable with what's been said so far, it's a fair bet this question has produced some sort of reaction in you. After all, *God* is such an emotive word, isn't it? So full of connotations of all different sorts.

Thankfully most people have moved past the clichéd view of a kind old man with a long white beard and flowing robes sitting atop a fluffy cloud. But the idea of God that's inherent in most mainstream forms of Christianity, Judaism and Islam is of some sort of spiritual being essentially *outside* of us, who has power over us and to whom we should be utterly dedicated. Even in the twenty-first century we still find the media debating 'why does God allow bad things to happen?'

Do you feel uncomfortable with this idea of a controlling, judgmental and all-powerful God?

Maybe you've rejected it because you feel it detracts from your personal responsibility for your *own* life, or because traditional scriptures don't seem relevant to the modern world? Perhaps you've rejected orthodox religion, for this and other reasons, but you retain a broadly spiritual outlook? As a minimum maybe you'd still say you believe in a God of some sort, you're just not sure *what* sort?

What if God isn't a person or being of some sort, but more of a concept?

Even in the aforementioned religions, words like *ineffable* and *unknowable* may be applied to God. These hint at the very inability of mere words to describe, and of human minds to fathom, the depths of something that's far better thought of as a concept than a being.

Can modern science help us here?

Yes. Many of us are already familiar with the story of how, when the scientists of the twentieth century started to delve more deeply into the insides of atoms, they found that electrons and protons and so on aren't really particles at all. They behave more like energy waves, also referred to as 'quanta'. So at the most fundamental level everything is made of pure energy.

A note of caution should be sounded at this point, in that any attempt to apply these discoveries to the spiritual arena is fraught with problems. This is because there are many more areas of fundamental disagreement over the correct interpretation of the theory than some 'quantum mystics' would have you believe.

One of these involves the extent to which behavior at the quantum level still applies as systems become more complex or 'entangled'. Or, to put it more simply, as we move up the scale from atom to molecule to complete organism or object, and so on. And the answer is almost certainly 'not very much', whichever interpretation of quantum theory you favor. So is the chair you're sitting on, or the bed you're lying on, or the floor you're standing on, physical and real? Perhaps an ascended master might be able to defy the apparent laws of physics by passing their hand clean through it, but most of us aren't quite there yet. We shouldn't, therefore, get too carried away with all this.

Yet it's still true that no matter how physically the molecules that come together to make you or your chair and so on might currently be expressing themselves, they're still basically made up of packets of energy. Everything is.

Can the Eastern religions, such as Hinduism and Buddhism, help us here too?

Indeed they can, despite some of them having pantheons of apparently human or animal gods. Because what they've long understood is that the ultimate deity isn't something external to us at all. It's *internal, in* everything. This idea is also found in the more esoteric forms of the Western religions such as Christian Mysticism, Kabbalism and Sufism, and in most native tribal worldviews.

These various approaches use a range of words to describe this more internal concept, such as the *Absolute*, *Universal* or *Ultimate*. They also tend to regard it as the ultimate creative power, so terms like *Origin* or *Source* are used as well. Hopefully you'll now have little trouble in associating this concept with that of the metaverse discussed earlier. By contrast some people find the next step a bit of a challenge, at least in the first instance. Yet if the best way to think of God is as the energy that underpins the entire universe and everything in it, there's only one conclusion that can sensibly be drawn... it's that *we are all God*.

Does this idea make you uncomfortable?

If it does, is it because you feel such a statement makes too great a claim for the human species, with all its wars, greed, materialism and so on? That's perfectly understandable.

But think of it this way. We're not only saying that we humans are all God. We're saying that *everything* in the universe is God, no matter how large or small, animate or inanimate, seen or unseen. Because it's *all* made up of the same energy of the one Source. How much better does that feel?

are we all One, and is everything just an illusion?

Two words that are also used to describe this ultimate, universal consciousness are the *All* or *One*. And these move us in a somewhat new direction.

The New Age movement that flowered in the sixties ushered in an awareness of more Eastern spiritual concepts, in particular those of reincarnation and karma. Over time these ideas have entered the mainstream, and we'll discuss them properly in part two.

But a number of more recent trends have tended to move the focus away from the individual and towards the view that everything is part of 'All That Is'. Revelations of this 'cosmic unity' lie at the heart of most transcendental experiences, and are commonly reported by those who enter altered states of awareness – whether via meditation, hallucinogens or, if you're really lucky, spontaneous moments of pure insight.

This increasing focus on unity has been reinforced by the speculations of quantum mystics, any by those who entreat us to harness the 'power of now' and shift to a more 'cosmic consciousness'. We'll discuss all these ideas later too.

One of the by-products of all this is the emergence of a view that's increasingly bandied about, and not just in more intellectual circles. It's the common adage that 'it's all just an illusion'. Yet there's good reason to suppose that, as a trend, this preoccupation with illusion has the potential to be at best misleading, and at worst even harmful – precisely because of the multitude of misconceptions that surround the word.

So what do we mean by 'illusion'?

To the extent that it simply means there's far more to life than just the physical world we see around us, there can be no real argument. After all this was the subject of the opening question.

But there are several more far-reaching views of illusion concerning, for example, the reincarnation cycle, or the notion of soul individuality – and we'll return to these shortly. Yet at the same time we often hear people talking about learning *lessons* and gaining *experience* so that their soul can *grow*, perhaps over many lives.

The key point is that all these viewpoints at least partially contradict each other. Indeed it's the resolution of these conflicts that lies at the heart of the concept of the holographic soul.

So can we bring the ideas of 'experience' and 'illusion' together?

We can draw a line bounded at one end by the concept of individual souls gaining experience, and at the other by the concept of illusion and unity with All That Is. And we can propose that any spiritual seeker will have a view of life that effectively places them somewhere along this 'experience-illusion line'. The idea of showing it at the base of a pyramid is that in large part the concept of the holographic soul can bring these various views together, as we'll see in due course.

the holographic soul
• experience *and* illusion • individuality *and* unity
• duality *and* nonduality

the experience-illusion line

experience   illusion
• individuality   unity •
• duality   nonduality •

The diagram also mentions the concept of 'nonduality', which is equally in vogue at the moment, and equally misunderstood. It refers to the fact that at some fundamental level there exists a 'unified' state of consciousness in which the distinction between apparent opposites, such as light and dark and so on, no longer exists.

Now it's true that any spiritual seeker might increasingly strive to achieve a more unified perspective on life, as we'll discuss in part two. But adopting an *entirely* nondual perspective is arguably only possible in the light realms. By the same token it's an impossibility while on the earth plane precisely because this is *designed* to be dualistic.

So those who are more experience oriented don't tend to see the duality of human life as an illusion to be seen through, but more as a deliberate condition created to allow us to experience the full range of human emotions. These are by their very nature dualistic: love and hate, happiness and sorrow, and so on.

Where would you place yourself on the experience-illusion line at the moment?

Those leaning towards the left side will tend to believe we incarnate in order to gain experience, and perhaps only have a limited appreciation that we're also part of All That Is. And they may or may not believe in the idea that we have many lives. Perhaps that's you?

Meanwhile we've already indicated that those leaning more towards the right are more complex. They cover a variety of positions because of the various approaches to illusion, and more indirectly to reincarnation, but what follows are the most obvious streams of thought.

Some take the idea of illusion to mean that there's no such thing as individualized soul consciousness at all. They would argue that any sense of individuality you might feel, even right now as an incarnate human being, is merely an illusion of separateness generated by your ego. Perhaps *that's* you?

Others might accept there's such a thing as an individual soul that reincarnates, but believe that fundamentally the cycle of death and rebirth is just an illusion. In other words, that as soon as we see through this illusion we escape from the chains that bind us to the 'karmic wheel', and reunite with Source. Such people may also tend to dismiss the idea of gaining experience – or at most they might place it purely in the context of dispelling the illusion, rather than of soul growth. Perhaps *that's* you?

Others again tend to reverse this. That is, they might accept that we exist as individual souls attempting to gain experience, but don't believe in any sort of individual soul continuity from one life to the next. In other words, they say, when you die there'll be no continuation of anything individually identifiable as 'you'. Perhaps *that's* you?

So what's the big deal here?

The reason these distinctions are so important is that each of these approaches tends to generate a distinctly different outlook on how we might live our lives. Or at least they should if their followers are thinking logically about the position they've adopted, and properly putting it into practice.

So to what extent should we be in pursuit of experience? Or aiming for transcendence and enlightenment? Or trying to see through the illusion of separateness and to rise above the world of duality? Or attempting complete non-attachment and surrender?

We'll talk more about all these ideas, and seek answers to all these questions, in part two. But to do so sensibly we must first understand more about the concept of the holographic soul itself, and how it attempts to bring these various streams of thought together into one coherent worldview.

in what way are our souls holographic?

The first part of the definition of the holographic soul runs as follows:

> Soul consciousness is holographic. We are both individual aspects of Source, and full holographic representations of it, all at the same time. However this does not mean that soul individuality is in itself an illusion. The principle of the hologram is that the part contains the whole, and yet is clearly distinguishable from it.

It's true that since its discovery the concept of the hologram has been applied to a variety of metaphysical ideas. So we hear of the 'holographic universe', or of 'holographic memory', and so on and so forth. These are all useful constructs.

But arguably it's only when the concept is applied to soul consciousness itself that it fulfills its greatest spiritual potential. And the reason for this is encapsulated in the final sentence of the definition above: 'The principle of the hologram is that the part contains the whole, and yet is clearly distinguishable from it.' In the current context this is crucial, because it allows us to conclude that soul individuality is *not* an illusion, while at the same time maintaining the inviolate principle of cosmic unity.

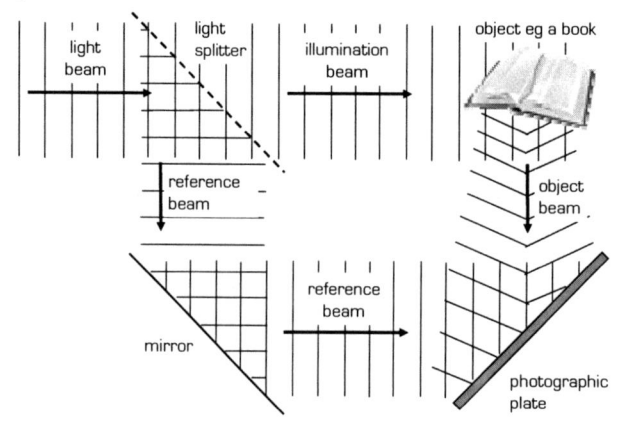

A proper understanding of this does require a small amount of simple holographic theory. But please don't be put off. This needn't be painful at all, especially with the aid of a simple diagram.

A basic hologram is created by shining a light beam through a 'splitter' angled at forty-five degrees. Some of the light carries straight on through as an 'illumination beam' that lights up all sides of an object, for example a book. An 'object beam' is then reflected off this at a forty-five-degree angle onto a 'photographic plate' placed at a similar angle.

At the same time the light splitter produces a 'reference beam' that's bounced off a mirror angled at forty-five degrees, and then onto the plate, creating an interference pattern.

Whenever the plate is subsequently illuminated by the original reference beam, a holographic, three-dimensional image of the original object is created in its original position, even when the object itself is no longer actually there.

But the crucial aspect for our purposes is that the photographic plate can be broken into increasingly small fragments, and *each one* will still reproduce the *entire* image – albeit with a slight loss of clarity at the extremes. And this is what's meant by 'the part contains the whole and yet is clearly distinguishable from it'.

Formulating the interplay between individual and universal soul consciousness in this way generates a number of profound insights, not all of which may yet be apparent, One of the most awe-inspiring is the implication that our individual soul consciousness encapsulates the entirety of the universal consciousness of Source, including memory, understanding, everything. And although it's something of a stretch for our human brains, the same must logically be true of every single element of the universe, even down to the quantum level.

The difference with humans, of course, is the extent to which we have a coherent, thinking consciousness. Our most enquiring minds have always intuitively understood that such limitless data and indeed wisdom exists. That's why philosophers, alchemists and spiritual seekers from across the ages have been preoccupied with the ultimate quest of how to access it.

why is the universe here at all?

This is clearly the most fundamental question of them all. It's also one that some who are more illusion oriented tend to avoid, perhaps suggesting that it's beyond our comprehension or remit. Sometimes there's even a hint that merely to ask it is to miss the point entirely. But does such a façade of apparent wisdom mask underlying contradictions that are being ignored?

Let's put it another way. Is it philosophically elegant to have such a 'cut-off point', beyond which we dare not venture? Surely the whole reason we humans have been given at least some intelligence and natural curiosity is to be forever searching for answers to ever more challenging questions?

More importantly this question is crucial to our development of a worldview that not only combines all the various streams of thought, but also places them in the fullest possible context – and therefore might, just might, take us closest to the truth. Of course we have to accept that anything we say about existence at this fundamental level can only be an approximation of the underlying reality. But should this be used as an excuse for not tackling the question at all?

What do you think? Shall we ask it anyway, to see what happens?

The point has already been made that one test of philosophical elegance is the simplicity of any solution. And here again we find a perfectly simple answer has been provided by a number of spiritual sources both ancient and modern.

The basic aim of Source itself is *to experience all that is and can be*. And it's only by the One becoming the many that there can be anything around to gain and reflect this experience.

To put this into context, here is the second part of the definition of the holographic soul:

> The primary aim of Source, in diversifying into all the billions of holographic soul aspects of itself that operate in the various realms throughout the universe, is to experience all that is and can be. So as individualized aspects of Source who have chosen to reincarnate on this planet, we are merely fulfilling a small part of that objective by gaining a balance of the experiences available via this route.

So on the one hand our separation from Source is indeed, at least partly, an illusion. In fact we can now see that the whole idea of reuniting with Source makes little sense if we never really left it in the first place. Moreover we have an interesting new twist to the atheist view that God is 'merely' the creation of man – because what's actually happening is that our experiences, and those of every other holographic aspect of Source throughout the universe, are continuously and automatically being fed back into it.

But at the same time this separation is real, and indeed essential. Without it we – as human souls for example – could never even have embarked on the process of gaining experience using our free will, and without 'knowing all the answers' in advance.

But why does Source bother to experience when it's already perfect?

This is a fascinating question that, once again, turns out to have a genuinely simple answer. Source is perfect, always. But how can it appreciate its own perfection if it's never experienced imperfection?

As holographic aspects of Source the same is true of all of us, of course. If all we ever did as souls was hang around in the light, basking in its unconditional love, we'd have the *knowledge* of what that love felt like but we wouldn't *appreciate* it, because we'd have no basis for comparison. It's only by forsaking and temporarily forgetting that bliss that we get to see the dark *and* the light amidst the often harsh realities of life on planet earth, and thereby start to gain a degree of *wisdom*.

Yet if we can grow to the point where we *do* remember who we really are, and start to strive for that bliss while still incarnate, *then* we're on our true path.

Does each of us have to experience absolutely everything on behalf of Source, in all possible combinations and permutations?

No, that would take an infinite number of lives and be philosophically inelegant. Nevertheless the aim for each of us is to experience a wide variety of circumstances that keep us moving towards – or more accurately *back* to – perfect love. And for each of us the outward and homeward journeys are different and unique.

So what does all this mean?

The concept of the holographic soul resolves most of the potential conflicts we discussed previously. In diagrammatic terms it places us pretty much in the centre of the experience-illusion baseline of our pyramid. It indicates that we're both full representations of Source and individual souls all at the same time. It indicates that we should be concerned with both duality and nonduality, each in their proper place. And it indicates that, while at times it may be useful to regard existence as illusory and part of a 'grand play' of cosmic theatre, the basic aim of gaining experience is real and fundamental.

The only issue that remains to be resolved is whether or not reincarnation should form part of this combined, all-encompassing worldview.

do we have many lives?

Have you ever thought about the conundrum of how people can have massively contrasting lives?

Consider the orphaned child living on the streets, deprived of any kind of love, affection or material comfort during a short, brutal and miserable life. Now compare this to the pampered aristocrat, born into a financial and emotional security of which the orphan couldn't even dream.

Can you explain that?

Is it just random chance? Or the vagaries of a capricious God? If you go down either of these routes, have you ever dared to think about them properly? Are you ever nagged by a feeling that your explanation is really rather empty, or even philosophically inelegant?

Whatever your intuitive or analytical reaction to the idea of reincarnation, there can surely be no denying that it presents the most logical and satisfying solution to *this* conundrum at least.

The idea is simple. Each of us will switch between all kinds of lives: from rich to poor; from loved to spurned; from man to woman; from long to short; from happy to sad; from celebrated to ignored; from clever to ignorant; from gentle to brutal; from loving to cold; and so on and so forth, including a variety of shades of grey in between.

The good news, for those of us who like our views grounded in evidence, is that again there's plenty of it to support the idea that we have many lives.

Admittedly not all of this evidence is as strong as some spiritual commentators suggest. Many seem to remain blissfully ignorant of the incredible power of the human mind to store every piece of information it ever receives, even if most of this is only retrievable in an altered state of consciousness. Hypnosis subjects with a vivid imagination can concoct what appear to be incredibly convincing past-life narratives, vividly replete with strange voices and accents, intense emotions and so on.

In some cases experiments seem to have proved that the subject's memories merely represented a jumble of information obtained by perfectly normal means in *this* life, even if they were only exposed to the information for a fleeting moment and retained no conscious memory of it at all.

But there remain a hard core of cases, involving both children and adults, where memories of past lives have thrown up detailed, factual information *so* obscure that at the very most only a handful of living people could have known it, if that. There are similarly strong cases involving near-death experiences, which provide evidence for the survival of consciousness in general.*

These most robust cases simply cannot be explained away by the simplistic arguments of skeptics. Indeed their dismissals are generally so illogical and reductionist that it seems they're the ones desperately clinging to a worldview that runs entirely contrary to the mounting evidence from various fields of research.

But can these apparent past-life memories come from some sort of central repository?

Many spiritual sources refer to a 'universal memory', sometimes called the 'collective unconscious' or 'akashic records'. But is it reasonable to suggest that apparent past-life memories aren't our own at all, but those of other souls retrieved from this shared database?

Sometimes this may indeed be the case. But thousands of subjects have now been regressed not just into *past* lives but into the time *between* lives.* We'll discuss this more in part two, but for now this 'interlife' research provides strong evidence of individual soul continuity. That's to say, it seems overwhelmingly likely that each of us does indeed have many lives that can be sensibly thought of as our own.

Yet how can there be enough souls when the world's population has been expanding so rapidly?

The first thing to remember is that, if we shorten the time interval between incarnations, the same number of souls can sustain a larger population. And some spiritual sources suggest this has increasingly been the case.

More important, human life on earth is only one small part of the universal story, even if it may be a relatively unique one. The evidence suggests there are many more planets, both physical and nonphysical, where we can gain experience. So the 'stock' of souls is universal, not earth-specific. It's also likely that new souls continuously 'emerge' from Source to maintain the flow of life.

---

* See the Big and Little Books of the Soul for details of these cases.
* Current-, past- and between-lives regression is normally achieved by hypnosis, although other techniques can be used.

suggestions

This second part of the book comprises various suggestions about how we can make our theoretical understanding of the holographic nature of our soul work for us in practice.

Nearly all of them have been assembled from other spiritual writings, although some have been given a reasonably unique slant. Particular emphasis is placed on how our attitude to experience versus illusion might impact our approach to life.

Almost certainly this doesn't represent a definitive list, and some of the simpler elements will tend to be of most use to those who are relatively new to a spiritual path. But if it acts as a useful starting point for further contemplation it'll have served its purpose.

forget karma, experience is all that matters

There are so many ideas about karma. It's truly one of the most misunderstood concepts in spirituality.

What do you think karma means?

For most people it involves 'paying off debts', 'reaping what you sow' or 'what goes around comes around'. And these ideas have developed out of the traditional view of karma as some sort of 'law of action and reaction'.

So how does karma work within our current life?

Here the 'law of attraction' applies, and sometimes it can be nice and obvious. For example we all know someone who always has a negative outlook, and so seems to attract only bad luck. But of course it's not bad *luck* at all.

We've already briefly mentioned the idea that we create our own reality – or life experiences – with our thoughts, intentions and so on. We'll talk more about the *conscious* creation or deliberate direction of our life later. In the meantime, if we haven't yet learned to master that discipline, most of our reality will be created by our *subconscious* thoughts, of which we're rarely aware. And these thought patterns may well be so jumbled and contradictory that to understand the dynamics of how they feed through into the life we experience will usually be way beyond our comprehension.

Not only that but we're genuinely interacting with many other people who are creating *their* own realities as well. Indeed, together we're all involved in a unique, collectively created, shared and interactive experience. Its underlying workings are very, very complex. And that's why we're so often left wondering 'why the hell did *that* happen to me?'

What about karma from one life to the next? How does that work? For example if we kill someone will they come back and kill us in another life?

This is the most directly retributive notion of karma, and while it could happen – anything and everything is *possible* – such a direct reaction is highly unlikely. There are far more subtle ways of learning that killing someone is a bad idea. For example the guilt in that life alone may be sufficient.

Indeed regression evidence shows that the dynamics of the linkages between and across our various lives are infinitely complex.

Admittedly if someone has a strong phobia for example, then regressing them into a relevant past life may find its source. And the mere reliving of that event may produce catharsis, so that the emotions not properly expressed at the time are given an outlet and safely discharged.

But many cases are far, far more complex than this. So much so that the therapist can often be left clutching at straws as to the real dynamics of the healing process. However all that really matters in such cases is that the client, in their altered state, processes the experience as directed by their higher self or guides.*

How do we know if certain karma is from this life, or a past one?

Mostly we don't. Just think for a moment. Do people ever know why they lost a wonderful job? Or why a partner they loved so much left them? Or why they got a terrible illness? Sometimes we can see, with the benefit of hindsight, how something that was seriously distressing at the time turned out to be a positive turning point in our life. But just as often these things won't become properly clear until we're back in the light realms after death.

If the event is significant enough we may have *planned* it while in soul form *before* we were born, of which more later. Otherwise we'll have created it as we went along with our underlying thoughts and intentions. But which is it? For most of us, most of the time, none of this is clear cut.

What should be clear by now is that understanding the underlying 'dynamics of karma', especially *across* lives, is for the most part way beyond human comprehension. And if it's beyond our comprehension, how can we use it to guide our everyday life?

Can't we just concentrate on producing enough good karma to outweigh the bad?

This way of looking at life at least has the advantage that there's no need to understand what's gone before. But who decides what's 'good' or 'bad', 'positive' or 'negative'? In some cultures you can have as many wives as you like. Try it in the West and you'll get slapped round the face and a jail term. Who decides what constitutes moral behavior, and is their judgment in any sense objective?

* Our higher self is our underlying soul consciousness. Our spirit guides are those souls who help and direct us. They do this when we're in soul form between lives, and also in various ways when we're incarnate in human form, of which more later.

How about generating no more karma at all, of any sort?

This does get round the problem of distinguishing between good and bad. But is it really a useful approach?

It might be for anyone who accepts that the reincarnation cycle exists but at the same time believes it's fundamentally an illusion to be seen through. They might see their objective as to break the compulsion to return to work out unresolved karma. Meanwhile someone who thinks that soul individuality itself is an illusion might pursue the related goal of nonattachment – of which more shortly – because of their focus on their oneness with All That Is. Such people would, by definition, place themselves towards the far right of the experience-illusion line.

So how would we go about generating no more karma? Certainly the most foolproof method, and in many ways the easiest, would be separation from our fellow humans and prolonged meditation. This is also where ideas of transcendence and enlightenment tend to come into play. Of course it's still possible to pursue these two goals while fully involved in life, but it's far, far harder.

There's no doubt that for some people in some lives – or in some *parts* of some lives – prolonged isolation is going to feel right. It's also true that regular meditation and contemplation is highly recommended for *all* of us.

But the arguments in the first part of the book suggested that gaining experience is our most significant purpose. And although isolation is of course an experience in itself, experience is *primarily* gained via action – and in particular *inter*action with others. So arguably the goal of generating no more karma is no more appropriate than any other karma-related goal.

Ok, if we accept that karma isn't a very helpful concept, what's experience all about?

There are some suggestions that planet earth may be unique in the extent to which it provides a dualistic environment of intense emotions of all hues and flavors. It's the harsh, coarse proving ground in which our ability to work through and express these various emotions is developed and refined over many, many lives.

Regression evidence indicates that we all need to learn how to shift progressively away from fear-based emotions and attitudes such as impatience, guilt, shame, selfishness, humiliation, jealousy, anger, hatred and revenge towards more love-based ones such as patience, altruism, openness, understanding, forgiveness and acceptance. And in order to experience and understand them properly we need not only to feel them ourselves, but also to feel what it's like to have them directed at us by others.

As a crucial part of this process we, as souls, sometimes plan to face extremely difficult circumstances in our next life. So for example those who are disabled in some way, whether from birth or by 'accident', will almost certainly have chosen this precisely because it provides a terrific opportunity to learn – about humility, patience, empathy, resilience and so on. The same may well be true of those who care for them, while together they may provide an inspirational example to others.

Of course anyone who's experiencing an extremely challenging life may find it very difficult, if not impossible, to accept any suggestion that they chose the circumstances they find themselves in. They may even find their life *so* harsh and difficult that they end it prematurely. But regression evidence suggests that after a period of rest and counseling in the light realms they would have to return to face the same challenges, possibly in even more difficult circumstances. It also seems that in the main we only pick the challenges we have the soul strength and soul experience to face.

So is life just about our own emotional growth?

Absolutely not. Again the evidence suggests that as we grow in experience we might deliberately choose to have 'altruistic' lives, which are more designed to help those around us to grow. Severe disability might be one example.

But nowhere is this perhaps better demonstrated than in the loss of a young child. Almost certainly they'll have volunteered for such a short life in order to help their families to experience the emotions of grief and loss at their sharpest, to reflect more deeply about life and death issues, and hopefully to pass this sternest of tests with dignity and love – not with anger, bitterness, resentment and self-pity.

But how does the concept of non-attachment found in many Eastern approaches fit into all this?

We've already seen that those whose beliefs place them to the far right of the experience-illusion line might aim to detach themselves from full involvement in earthly life, perhaps by complete isolation.

By contrast those who are more experience oriented might tend to see this as largely a wasted opportunity. But non-attachment doesn't have to be this extreme. It might be that we involve ourselves fully in the experiences of life, and yet still aim to find ourselves becoming less and less attached to particular events and their outcomes. In other words, we might learn to react to the apparently good and bad with equal inner calm, accepting that life will ebb and flow – albeit that strong emotions can have their place.

We've also seen that the underlying dynamics of any situation often take time to understand. So something that might initially appear favorable may eventually turn out to be less so, and vice versa. Can you think of any examples of this in your own life?

Most Eastern approaches also contain the concept of 'impermanence'. That is, they caution us that nothing lasts forever, and that everything changes. So for example the person who's on the up will usually have to be ready for some sort of fall at some point – unless they've achieved full spiritual mastery over their life – while someone down on their luck can usually look forward to better times ahead.

So is total non-attachment our ultimate goal?

In some ways yes, although we must be very careful what we mean by it. It certainly doesn't mean losing our humanity, or never having emotions, or cutting ourselves off from others. Yet we can broadly assume that it's exactly when we reach the point of having risen above earthly attachments in the right way that we've conquered its challenges, and are ready to move on from the reincarnation cycle.

What do we mean by 'the right way'? There's certainly a balance to be achieved between just 'being' and getting on and 'doing', which we'll return to later. But it should be clear by now that this cycle will only be completed when we've striven to properly work through all our emotional and other challenges.

We *could* attempt to skip all the hard stuff by removing ourselves from everyday life. But we've already seen that it's one thing to have mere *knowledge* of something, and quite another to fully experience it and achieve *wisdom* as a result. So it's highly likely that any transcendence or enlightenment achieved without the requisite hard graft of experience, interaction and involvement will only be a temporary *state*, and perhaps even illusory in its own right.

That's because there are no shortcuts to genuine *transformation*. It's a long-term *process* in which emotional mastery of a huge variety of experiences and situations is achieved over many lifetimes, leading finally to non-attachment *combined with* unconditional love. We might refer to this as 'loving non-attachment'.

Nor should we fall into the trap of making assumptions about how far down the transformation route we've progressed. Anyone who thinks they've made it, and this is their last life on earth, should probably beware. They may be in for something of a shock when they return home to the light.

strive to be motivated by love, not fear

Every single emotion originates in either love or fear. These are the two fundamental, emotional reactions that dominate everything we think, say and do. And it hardly needs emphasizing that we should all strive to bring love, not fear, into every aspect of our lives. This is one area where there's no disagreement, irrespective of where you place yourself on the experience-illusion line.[*]

But is this easier said than done? What about when someone annoys or insults us for example?

Let's say a fellow motorist gets annoyed at our driving, with little reason. They gesture rudely, their face contorted with rage. Do we react instantaneously with more of the same? Or do we take a deep breath, calm ourselves and remember: 'That's *their* dream. I don't need to take this personally.'

Let's not forget that we don't know the underlying dynamics of the situation either. Maybe their partner has just left them after twenty years of marriage. Imagine how *you* might feel in that situation.

Their rage is really nothing to do with us at all, so there's no need to react with equal venom. That would be the fear-based reaction, expressed as anger. Instead, why not imagine that their partner *has* just left them, and send them caring and compassionate thoughts? It may or may not do them much good, but it'll certainly be better for us.

In fact if any situation starts to provoke a fear-based reaction in us, whether it's anger, hatred, jealousy or whatever, we can ask ourselves this simple question: 'How can I look at this differently so I feel love instead?' And if we don't know the other person involved, we can *make something up* to explain their behavior, like they just lost their job or their partner just left them, or whatever we like. After a while we can even have fun with this by making up humorous things.

---

[*] Although the underlying thought process might be somewhat different. For example those who are more illusion oriented might bring love into every situation more due to their appreciation of the unity of everything than for reasons of personal growth.

People talking about focusing on the positives rather than the negatives in life, but how do we do that when so many bad things are happening?

Well, for a start we might make a deliberate effort to notice the teenager helping the old lady across the road; or the dog leading his blind owner; or the beauty of the snowflake on the window pane.

This doesn't mean blissfully ignoring the bad things in the world. But we shouldn't let them overwhelm us, and we should perhaps give them our attention only when we aim to do something to change them – by sending out love to those in distress for example. Otherwise we're just worrying and putting out negative thoughts to no constructive effect.

Another great approach is to remember to be grateful for what we *do* have, rather than bemoaning the lack of what we don't. So when we wake up we might give thanks that we have a warm bed, a roof over our head, hot water, food in the cupboards and so on.

More than this we can work at being grateful for *everything* that happens, and look to find the positive aspect of *any* and *every* situation. For example that traffic jam might have saved us from a disastrous crash. Losing our job could be the spur to make us start doing something we love for a living, or it might allow us to meet our soul mate in the job centre. If we train ourselves to trust in the flow of the universe, we'll start to see the potential for growth in everything.

Bringing love not fear to everything we think, say and do in these ways is incredibly good for us. Every time we do it we feel so much better about ourselves and about our life. And we'll be having a much wider impact too. Remember that stranger who smiled at you the other morning, instead of just walking on by engrossed in their own thoughts? How did that make you feel? When we bring love to someone else we have an impact on them too, and so on and so forth, like ripples in a pond.

But what if someone or something consistently gets to us? Can't we at least let our feelings out in private?

We all need to let off steam sometimes, whether just by ourselves, or to a close friend who knows this is merely a temporary release and not our normal, loving self.

But we should be wary here too. If a certain person or event repeatedly produces a fear-based reaction in us, it's a likely sign that we need to analyze what's really going on underneath. No matter how much we might want to blame someone else for our anger or frustration – our partner, for example – our reaction almost certainly points to there being something that *we* need to work through ourselves.

Remember too that we might think we've reached a point of total balance, but pride comes before a fall. It's pretty likely that sooner or later something or someone will come along that pushes another emotional button, or even one we thought we'd dealt with already. And so we go to work again. This is healthy, and all part of the growth process.

It's also worth remembering that every single thought has an impact, not just on the reality we create for ourselves, but also for humanity as a whole. All fear-based thoughts mount up on one side of the scales, all love-based ones on the other. And guess which side's been winning for a long while? It's time for a global shift in consciousness away from fear and towards love.

take personal responsibility for everything

The idea of life planning has already been mentioned several times. For anyone who supports the idea of individual soul growth over many lifetimes, it's the single most important finding of the research into the time between lives that various psychologists and psychiatrists began to stumble upon in the late sixties.

Although this work is more widely known now, in the first few decades the pioneers themselves remained ignorant of each others' findings, as did the general public who made up their subjects. That's why the underlying consistency of their thousands of reports – of transition and healing, of past-life reviews, of soul group interaction, of next life planning and of return – is so impressive and evidential.

But of all these aspects of the interlife, life planning is the one with the most far reaching implications. The evidence strongly suggests that most of us, as souls, are actively involved to a greater or lesser extent in choosing the circumstances of the next life we're going to have on earth.

Some subjects report that they merely know the bare bones, such as their sex and their parents' location and general circumstances. But others describe how spirit guides present them with several lives to choose from, and how they're able to watch each of them as if on a film that can be fast-forwarded and paused at any moment. They even suggest they can enter the scene to actually feel what that person's life is like.

Of course this brings us to another key question about which there's much confusion:

Are our lives all mapped out in advance?

The answer is an emphatic *no*. When interlife subjects describe these glimpses of their next life, they indicate that they represent major probabilities and lesser possibilities only. They aren't predetermined or set in stone. And the reason they're not is due to an inviolate principle that's stressed above almost all others in all the most profound spiritual writings. It also answers the oft-posed question of why, if we plan our lives in advance, we can't remember anything about this process. It's the fundamental principle of *free will*.

So the only way we can play our part in gaining useful experience on planet earth is to reincarnate with no memories of what we've planned, and to use our free will to make our own decisions at every fork in the road.

Sometimes we get help by agreeing certain 'triggers' that act as signposts along the way, even though we don't have the full map. Have you ever seen something unusual about someone – a physical feature, or an item of clothing, or something they were doing – that somehow seemed very familiar? Or just felt drawn to speak to a complete stranger for no obvious reason? These things are usually based on triggers agreed with the other person before incarnation.*

Most of the forks in the road will only be minor. But if we take a wrong turning at a major one our higher self or spirit guides will attempt to nudge us back on track via a variety of methods, of which more later.

So what does all this mean?

It means that, in the fullest sense, everything we *do* and everything we *experience* and everything we *are* is all down to our own choices and free will. It's down to all the choices we made in *previous* lives, which have combined to make our soul what it is now, with all its strengths and weaknesses. It's down to the specific choices we made when *planning* this life. And it's down to the choices we've made *within* this life, which have got us to where we are now because of the law of attraction – or our own creation of our own reality with our own thoughts and attitudes, whether consciously or subconsciously.

We might be tempted to blame others: 'If only my partner wasn't so lazy/was more loving/listened to me more/didn't nag me so much, my life would be so much better.' But who chose our partner? And who is continuing to choose to stay with them? Or we might be tempted to blame God: 'How can he allow me to suffer so terribly?' Or we might be tempted to blame our past karma: 'I must have done something really bad in a past life to be suffering as I am now.'

But there's a more courageous alternative by which we take full, personal responsibility and reap the rewards that brings: 'Everything I am has led me to where I am now. And I'm going to take complete control of my thoughts, intentions and desires, and take myself forward in exactly the direction I want to go.'

Of course this is more or less daunting depending on our emotional and financial situation, the extent to which we have dependants like

---

* Incidentally the most important relationships in life are not necessarily the longest, but the ones with the most impact. A brief encounter of only a few minutes might have a profound influence on our life. By contrast in any particular life our long-term partner for example might not be a soul mate at all.

children or elderly parents, and so on and so forth. And to bring about this fundamental shift takes time, and involves a number of other factors we haven't yet discussed.

But whatever our situation we can ask ourselves if we want to carry on hiding behind excuses? Or do we want to start taking responsibility and directing our life, even if it's only in small ways to begin with? Because this is an essential first step on the path to inner contentment.

Talking of which...

search for the contentment within

Do you remember when, as a child, you were so focused on having that one toy, whatever it might have been, that you felt your life would be horribly incomplete without it? As an adult do you still find yourself thinking that that new pair of shoes, or that new outfit, or that new haircut will make you happy? Or that new car, or house, or holiday?

But have any of these things *ever* brought you anything more than fleeting pleasure, followed by a burning desire to possess the next thing?

On the other hand, what about that sunset you watched the other day? Or the color and smell of those flowers? Or that birdsong?

How did these things make you feel, deep inside? And did they cost you, or the planet, anything?

But how can we find regular contentment when everything about modern life is so stressful?

People think stress arises from working too hard or something of that sort. But it doesn't. It stems from not being in control, and being at the mercy of others.

Admittedly there are lots of things in life we can't control, at least not fully. This includes the actions and reactions of other people – our partner, our family, our friends, our boss, our colleagues – all of whom are, or at least should be, controlling their own paths.

The one thing we can control, however, is ourselves. We can control what we choose to think about and how we think about it, and thereby control how we feel – knowing that this will help us to control how we react to others. This is always worth remembering when we feel stressed.

So how do we really find 'inner peace'?

This can't be achieved overnight. It takes time, and there are many pathways to it. What follows then are just some pointers.

Later we'll discuss how one of our goals in life should probably be to earn our living from something that really makes us feel good inside. But even before we achieve that, no matter how busy we are it's surely a good idea to make a special effort to spend enough time each day, or at least each week or month, doing at least one thing that gives us a sense of contentment. Again we can all agree on this, irrespective of where we are on the experience-illusion line. It isn't selfishness unless taken to extremes, and if others make it out to be we should remember that we're no use to those around us if we're not content within ourselves.

Preferably we should choose activities that genuinely feed our inner sense of peace and calm, rather than stressful sports or hobbies, or mere superficial and fleeting pleasures. Perhaps we'll get involved with that thing that little voice inside has been nagging us about for years – like taking up a musical instrument, or learning how to sail, or writing that book we've got inside us.

These don't have to be solitary pleasures. We can share the experiences, whatever they are, if we want to. But if we do we should work at remaining unaffected by any factors that might spoil our enjoyment, otherwise we're better off on our own. The key is that our contentment shouldn't *depend* on anyone or anything else at all.

All the pieces of advice in this part of the book go together of course, and none should be taken in isolation. So making time for meditation and contemplation comes into this too, as does facing up to our lower self, of which more later.

But we'll almost certainly find that the more we develop these habits and modes of being, the more we'll discover the inner peace, contentment and love that we all carry inside us as a birthright. We'll come to realize that everything we need is already inside us. How could it be otherwise when we're all holographic aspects of Source?

So give yourself time, and work on this inner contentment in whatever ways are best for you. One thing you might try is to regularly get yourself out into a natural setting, because this works better than anything else on just about everyone. Proper remote countryside is ideal, but even an inner city park can work wonders if your mindset is right.

And one day you'll find that a single, special moment in nature will reduce you to tears of the deepest joy, in a way that a thousand new shoes or cars or houses could never even approach.

You'll feel so alive, and so lucky to be here. And all you'll want to do is stretch out your arms, look up and say 'thank you'.

You may even, in time, achieve that elusive goal where you always see the world anew, like a child filled with awe at the wonder and beauty of it all. Every moment of our existence on this planet is, after all, a true miracle.

love yourself first

Does this sound selfish to you? If so you're taking it the wrong way. It isn't meant to be smug or self-satisfied, arrogant or preening. What if we said 'know yourself, and be comfortable in your own skin' instead? Does that sound better?

Of course if you've been on a spiritual path for some time you'll be very familiar with this advice. But how many of us really understand what it means?

Have you ever spent significant time alone, not in a relationship?

Perhaps not. Whenever a relationship ends, do you feel so great a *need* not to be alone that you have to be with someone else as soon as possible? In the internet age it's pretty simple.

Many people do behave like this. Even when they're alone, they're constantly thinking about finding someone new. They feel that if they're single they're somehow not complete. Maybe you know someone like that?

This is one of the reasons why the average length of relationships – whether marriages or not – is falling all the time. It's not only because women no longer have to stay when they're unhappy, which is clearly a good thing. It's increasingly because people rush from one relationship to the next, never waiting long enough for a genuinely compatible person, maybe even a true soul mate, to come along.

After all, it's so easy to be in love at the start, isn't it? But it's so easy for that love to fade too, especially if it's a relationship hastily embarked upon and only built on sand. And there's heartache, and recriminations, and children with yet more step-parents, and so on and so forth.

On the other hand, maybe you've been alone for a long time. But are you doing it bravely, and are you comfortable with it? That is, are you *really* comfortable with it? Or have you just given up because you don't want to get hurt any more? Or perhaps, deep down, you don't think you're worthy of anyone's love?

What should we be striving for then?

Loving relationships are our natural mode of being as humans. We're fundamentally sociable and loving beings who aren't designed to be alone.

Admittedly some people, in some lives, choose to have very few if any relationships. That's a choice and an experience open to anyone, and it sometimes attracts those who are more illusion oriented.

But when it comes to soul growth and emotional experience there's no greater pleasure, or greater challenge, than that offered by a long-term, loving relationship based on genuine respect and compatibility. And of course having children provides the supreme proving ground for unconditional love.

So why do some of us keep attracting the wrong sort of partner?

The law of attraction comes into play in relationships just as in anything else. Indeed it's usually more obvious here than elsewhere, especially to outside observers who aren't caught up in the emotional drama.

This doesn't necessarily mean we attract a partner with the exact same character traits as us, although occasionally we might. What it does mean is that we often attract someone at roughly the same stage of emotional development. The emotions each of us is working on will probably be different, yet complementary enough that if we get it right we can learn what we need from each other. But if both of us are carrying plenty of unresolved baggage it can get very messy.

For example maybe one partner is really needy, while the other is cold and unloving. Maybe the first one subconsciously thrives on being rejected. Of course consciously they'd say that's nonsense, how could anyone *want* what they keep going through. But deep down they don't love themselves so they don't expect anyone else to either, and they attract partners who'll fulfill that belief for them. Yet if they're brave enough to concentrate on their *own* shortcomings, these partners offer them the chance to recognize and grow out of old, ingrained habits.

We get what we expect to get, remember? But it's what we expect *deep down*, not on the surface, that counts. So the best approach of all is to do some digging, and get all that unresolved emotional stuff sorted out, *before* we start trying to be in a relationship with anyone. Otherwise we'll simply attract someone else with similar amounts of baggage.

What if you love your partner yet still feel unfulfilled. What if somehow they don't make you happy?

If you feel this way you'd do well to ask yourself, 'why should they'? It's the same as with houses, cars, clothes and so on. Perhaps you think that if only you could find 'the one' it would make you blissfully happy. But each partner turns out *not* to be the one, no matter how wonderful things were at the start. So you keep on searching or longing because you've forgotten that other important maxim... real contentment only comes from *within*.

So we should be careful not to expect a partner to make us happy. That's *our* job, no one else's. And until we sort it out *nothing* is going to give us genuine inner calm and contentment. By the same token we shouldn't make the mistake of thinking that our partner's happiness is our responsibility. It's not, it's *theirs*.

And if it comes to the point, long term, where we're doing our bit but they're not doing theirs, arguably it's time to pull out and move on. Not with recriminations, regrets and bitterness, but with gratitude and love.

meditate regularly and develop your intuition

We all know about that still, small voice inside us. Listening to our intuition, our instincts, our gut feel, our heart not our head, or whatever we want to call it, is the first step on the path to a more rounded spiritual life. It's also the easiest step, because we can all do it. It's just a case of developing the skill and *trusting* it.

The reason this is so important is that our intuition is the primary means by which our spirit guides and higher self communicate with us. There are plenty of other mechanisms, including intervening in our dreams, but these messages aren't always so easy to pick up.

What about coincidences, or 'synchronicities'?

These are another hugely popular way of getting us to wake up to something, so it's always important to pay attention to them. Although it's easy to get carried away with this when we first start to open up, it's true that everything, no matter how small, tends to happen for a reason.

So how can we develop our intuition?

There's really only one, obvious way. It's to follow the essential advice given by all the most profound sources of spiritual wisdom... that is, to meditate regularly each day, even if only for a few minutes. Meditation opens up our channels to our higher self and guides, and allows us to start to access the limitless wisdom that's our birthright as a full holographic representation of Source.

But what if we're so busy we just can't find the time to meditate regularly?

It's all about priorities. If we really want to and it's important enough we can make time, instead of excuses. We can start off with just five minutes a day, and even if we never get beyond that it's better than no minutes at all. But we almost certainly will go further, as we not only come to enjoy the experience but to miss it if we don't do it.

Fine. Yet for some of us the real problem is that we've tried it and we find it difficult.

Why is it so hard? Why can't we switch our brain off?

Everybody struggles with this. Even when you've been doing it for a long time, sometimes you still struggle. But guess what? We don't have to be perfect. Making the effort is what counts here.

Not only that, but switching our brain off completely so that we think of nothing at all doesn't have to be our aim. Only the most advanced practitioners – perhaps those who are more illusion oriented – strive to empty their mind completely for any length of time. For the rest of us there are all sorts of approaches that don't require this, which can be used for many different purposes.

Can we chant affirmations to ourselves during a meditation?

Yes. This tends to automatically empty our mind of distracting thoughts and help us to focus inwards. Affirmations are at their most powerful when they're ones we've taken the time to think about for ourselves rather than just following what someone else tells us. Our higher self, guides and anyone else who might be listening in know the difference between something being recited by rote and something that contains genuine feeling and desire.

So most obviously we might develop affirmations that relate specifically to our goals and aspirations at this time in our life. But we can also include requests to our higher self to help us with the general things discussed throughout this part of the book. For example to bring our higher self more to the fore; to do everything we do out of love; to generate our contentment from within; to be of service to others; and to maintain a positive outlook.

What about specific problems?

It's when we concentrate on a particular problem that's troubling us that meditation becomes rather more like prayer. But simplistically at least there's a difference. Because instead of just passively asking our higher self or guides for *help* and then shutting down, in meditation we can actively ask for *advice* and then *stay quiet* to see if anything comes through – perhaps as an image, or a feeling, or even in specific words.*

It might not of course, but we shouldn't be put off. Sometimes we aren't open enough to hear them properly at the time, so they may get our answer through later and in another way. In a dream for example, or via one or more synchronicities.

So do we need to adopt some special cross-legged position that feels

---

* Whether help and advice comes from our higher self or guides is unimportant, because to some extent they're interchangeable when we're in human form. What matters is to be open and to listen to it.

really uncomfortable?

Absolutely not. The details of what we do genuinely don't matter. It's all about the intention to contemplate, go within and hook up with our higher self or guides. If we want to follow some of the more advanced Eastern practices, that's fine. But they're not essential.

So if you want to meditate cross-legged, do it. If you want to meditate lying on your back on your bed or on the floor, do it – although make sure you're not tired, otherwise you'll just fall asleep. If you want to meditate naked standing on your head... well, that's entirely up to you.

But don't we have to do special breathing?

Not really. All that matters is that we're comfortable and relaxed, and that our breathing is deep and regular. It might be helpful to count slowly to four on the intake and again during exhalation, at least to start with. Again this helps us to focus inwards.

If we want to go further then at some point we might like to practice breathing with our stomach rather than our chest, pushing it out on the intake and sucking it back in as we exhale, making for a kind of cyclical or circular motion. But it's not essential. In the first instance we should try to keep it simple and natural, and not to weigh ourselves down with lots of rules.

Is there anything else we need to know about meditation?

Although we really don't want to get too bogged down at the outset, in time there are a number of useful little nuances we can add into our meditation practice.

The first is some sort of healing. We can imagine a brilliant, intense, white light – perhaps like that at the centre of the sun – coming in through the top of our head, or through our solar plexus, then filling our entire body and the aura around it. We can visualize it dispelling any negative or darker energy and replenishing us with pure light.

The second, which is related, is some form of white light protection to safeguard us from unwanted energies – not only as we open ourselves up during meditation, but also in our everyday life. We can imagine the light encircling us to form a protective bubble, or a shell, or whatever image works best.

Finally there's another genuinely important spiritual practice that should ideally become a habit, and making it part of our regular meditation, perhaps at the end, can ensure that. We've touched on this already – it's to always remember to give thanks for what we have. Gratitude is a hugely powerful emotion.

So even when life feels pretty miserable, it's worth trying really hard to think about the things we might be grateful for. Even if the situation seems desperate and we're all alone, with money worries and goodness knows what else, there *will* be something positive if we search for it. It might just be some personal character trait – resilience, or being kind and loving – or it might be our child or children, or anything. We have to try to find *something* that we're proud of and can hang onto.

If we let that be our inspiration, and give thanks for it even when our world seems to be collapsing around us, our gratitude at that moment will surely repay us a thousand times over.

drop the mask and face up to your lower self

We've already seen that we can't be in a genuinely balanced, spiritually mature relationship until we've put in the hard work to get rid of our baggage. And that we can't approach loving non-attachment unless we've worked through a whole range of emotional lessons and mastered them.

And these things *don't happen overnight*. They take whole lifetimes, indeed many lifetimes, and what they require above all else is proper introspection and analysis. Of course professional therapy and regression are available to clear serious blockages or to act as catalysts to speed up the process, but the more we develop the more we'll be able to use various self-help techniques. For example self-regression into childhood or even previous lives during meditation can be an extremely powerful tool. It can reveal situations and intense emotions completely foreign to our normal, conscious memory.

So what is the 'lower self', and the 'mask'?

Whatever approach is taken, one of the fundamental tasks of any true spiritual seeker is to face up to the lower or shadow self. This comprises the bits of ourselves we prefer to hide, pretending they're not there. They will usually be more fear-based emotional aspects that we haven't yet conquered – either as a leftover from a previous life, or as a new challenge in this one. And not only do we hide them from ourselves, but we wear a mask in public in the hope that other people won't see them either.

But of course if we're going to genuinely love and know ourselves we've got to face these less desirable, or less developed, aspects of our personality. We need to acknowledge them bravely, but also in a balanced way. So in order to remove the fear that the whole false edifice of our life will come tumbling down if we do face them, at the same time we should make sure we actively remind ourselves of those areas where we're strongest – that is, our more developed traits.

And it's always worth remembering that we're not alone, and can ask our higher self and guides for help *at any time*. It's also useful to keep a diary to record our progress and insights.

In this way we gradually learn to see ourselves as we really are, no better and no worse, without turning away in fear and disgust. More than this, eventually we'll be able to cast off the mask and then, solid and confident in our own foundations, we can face other people without it. Authentically. As we truly are. And without fear of their reaction or their judgment.

But aren't we supposed to forego introspection and instead 'live in the now', or be 'fully present in the moment'?

This is one of the most popular pieces of advice with those who are more illusion-oriented, and it's found in many modern spiritual books. But it's worth emphasizing that *all* the most profound spiritual sources carry exactly this message.

Why? Firstly living in the now stops us endlessly worrying about a past that's over and cannot be changed, and about a future that hasn't even happened yet. It also encourages us to take time out to appreciate what we have and what we're experiencing, right here, right now, rather than always assuming that some future thing – a new relationship, house and so on, all the things we've already discussed – will make us happy. All this is to the good.

But is living in the now the be-all-and-end-all of our spiritual quest?

No. The extent to which the modern proponents of living in the now actually suggest this depends on how far to the right of the experience-illusion line they are, which isn't always entirely clear. But what's clear is that many followers of this advice seem to take it that way. Yet we've seen that for experience-hungry individual souls it's essential to engage in a degree of thoughtful introspection if we're to confront our lower self and grow.

Can the related exhortation to 'quieten the mind' be harmful if misunderstood?

If we take from this the idea that somehow our mind is our enemy – whether or not that's what the advice is really saying – then yes it can, and perhaps we need to think again. Our mind is *only* our enemy to the extent that we let it run away with and dominate us with an endless stream of worries and cares that may or may not, but often do, amount to nothing. On the other hand our mind is very important, indeed essential, to the process of introspection, and of learning who we really are so we can grow.

Why is living in the moment so hard to do consistently?

Only those who are genuinely ready to quit the reincarnation cycle, because they've put in all the hard work, will be able to live in the now and practice loving non-attachment as a permanent state of being. And we need to be clear that at any one time most of us are *not* in that lofty position, however much we might like to think otherwise. So it's a very good idea to practice living in the moment, but we shouldn't get too frustrated if we find it somewhat challenging.

What's more, hopefully we can now agree that for most of us it would be a mistake to concentrate unduly on living in the now at the expense of facing up to our lower self. Yet this will be just as challenging. It takes guts and perseverance. It can also take a long time, because our persona is like an onion and has a lot of layers. We've already mentioned that whenever we think we're sorted out we'll be fine for a while, until another challenge comes along to test us and reveal more about the work we still have to do. But that's fine. That's how it's supposed to work.

Above all, no matter how difficult this introspection process may be, it's the only approach that'll allow us to *see* who we really are, to *be* who we really are, and to *grow* into who we really can be.

consciously create the future you desire

We've already repeatedly mentioned the idea that we create our own reality. That is, our thoughts and intentions shape what happens to us.

And we've seen that the key factor is this: do we allow this process to be largely governed by our *subconscious*, so that we're reactively battered by the apparent 'slings and arrows of outrageous fortune'? Or do we make the decision to be proactive, and take control of the process with *conscious* intent?

Of course the latter is the favored course of action, and the one recommended by a plethora of modern self-help books. However a note of caution is again required.

Is the 'secret' of conscious creation really as easy as they say?

Any approach that suggests we can have *anything* we want at *any* time just by focusing hard enough on it will leave many of us sadly disillusioned with the whole process. We may be left wondering whether we did something wrong, maybe even thinking somehow we're a failure.

The hard truth is that we'll only be able to consciously create on a consistent basis once we've got rid of the bulk of our lower-self baggage. Until that time our conscious desires will often be thwarted by conflicting messages from our subconscious, which are stronger, and which we remain blissfully unaware of until we decide to face them.

So again there are no short-cuts to this. We've got to put the work in to reap the rewards.

Assuming we've put in this underlying effort, what's the best way to make conscious creation work? How specific should we be for example?

There's conflicting advice about this. Some say we should be as specific as possible about the outcomes we desire, even down to being exact about the date by which we expect something to happen. Others suggest that the more flexible we are, especially about the *means* by which an outcome might be achieved, the more we give our higher self and guides – indeed the universe in general – some room for maneuver.

The answer probably lies in a balance between the two. If we're too vague the universe hasn't got a clue what we really want. If we're too specific, especially if we expect something to happen yesterday, we're not giving it a chance.

Probably the best advice is to be as firm as we can in defining what we really want as a *final* outcome, without concerning ourselves with the possible alternative routes *to* that outcome. So we should try to focus on the 'what', not the 'how'. As to the 'when' we can leave that open unless we feel very strongly that we must put a time limit on a particular outcome.

Should we write our desired outcomes down?

Yes, almost certainly this is a good idea. It's best if we phrase them in the present tense as if they've already happened, and positively by concentrating on what we do want rather than what we don't. All these things will ensure our affirmations of them are much more powerful.

We can also put them up on a 'vision board' with accompanying pictures and, as suggested previously, use them as affirmations in our meditations. In fact we can affirm them at any time. When we're traveling, exercising, waiting in a queue – any time we feel it's appropriate. This can only help to reinforce them.

And as already suggested at some point one of our goals, probably even the main one, should be to do something we love for a living. 'Follow your bliss', as they say.

Is there any other advice?

Yes. To work properly this really has to become a way of life for us, something we live by every day. We should always be enthusiastic about our desired outcomes, really picturing them in our head, and feeling the pleasure they give us. And if we truly feel that it's our destiny to be healthy, wealthy, successful, in love or whatever, irrespective of our current circumstances, then we will be.

Another crucial aspect of conscious creation is learning to spot negative thoughts creeping in, and to stop them in their tracks before they can sabotage us. This is one of the hardest parts to begin with, because most of us are so used to thinking negatively we don't even notice. But once we do spot them we mustn't allow ourselves to dwell on a past we can't change or a future that may never happen. Instead we can banish them straight away with a simple trigger word like 'cancel' or 'delete'.

It's also important to make our outcomes realistic enough that we really believe in them. If we start by aiming low we can get a few successes under our belt. Then as we gain in confidence we can start to push the boundaries. And there are no limits, just what we allow ourselves to believe and imagine.

But isn't this all rather me, me, me?

It can seem that way, can't it? The truth is this power can be used in any way we want. That's what free will is all about. So if we want to use it for entirely self-centered and material ends we may be perfectly successful sometimes. Having said that conscious creation will only work consistently if we're a relatively experienced soul who's done their groundwork. That being the case our motives are likely to be more altruistic anyway. Almost certainly being of service to others will increasingly become more important to us than serving our own selfish ends.

In a similar vein a fear-based approach in which our success is seen as *rivaling* that of others is likely to come to naught. But if we see it as merely augmenting that of others, and as a *cooperative* venture, this love-based approach has a far greater chance of bearing fruit.

So does being on a spiritual path mean we should live a life of poverty and deprivation?

Absolutely not. Our planet contains sufficient bounty and abundance for all, if only we would garner it wisely and share it more equally. Of course *undue* concentration on material trappings probably isn't conducive to spiritual growth. But nor is there any need for us to be self-conscious about wanting to create a comfortable life for ourselves and our loved ones.

After all, if you *have* put in all the hard work, and successfully faced the countless difficult tests of your many lives, then don't you deserve it?

But shouldn't we be careful what we wish for?

Probably. Some people see conscious creation on any widespread scale as being fraught with difficulty because we can't be sure if what we're aiming for is in line with our life plan.

For example, let's say we have a goal that we've been deliberately pursuing with all our conscious power, yet it never seems to come any closer. As a result we might assume that we haven't fully mastered the art of conscious creation, at least in this particular area, and that our subconscious must be sending out conflicting signals. If so we'd need to go back to the drawing board and search within for the source of these blockages.

But what if this introspection doesn't reveal any blockages? This might imply that this goal is, at least at this time, way off our life plan – and that our higher self and guides are doing what *they* can to block it. It might be that what appears to be a less than desirable experience is important for our growth, and something we chose to face.

So do we need to know what our life plan is before we can consciously create with any confidence?

Some people certainly feel we need to establish our life purpose in order to give our efforts at creation proper direction. But what might this be, and how might we establish it?

On the one hand it might be some major emotional lesson that we're working on, which might in itself take a great deal of introspection to establish. On the other we've already seen that the more experience we gain the more our purpose will shift towards altruism. So it might be more along the lines of using our skills in some way in the service of others. Those skills and the way we should use them will be unique for each of us, but if we stay open we can trust the universe to reveal them to us when the time's right.

But are there multiple elements to our life plan, and can we really know all of them?

Most of us will indeed have multiple aspects to our plan, related to both our own emotional growth and to more altruistic endeavors, and different aspects will be more or less important at different times. And to some extent they'll also change depending on how well we're progressing with our challenges, and how other people around us are getting on as well. As with most things it's a complex, dynamic process.

But don't we have an overall purpose that's different from our general plan?

We might like to think that our overall purpose is our ultimate destination, while our life plan is our journey to get there. But can we really distinguish between the two? The answer is probably not.

So where does that leave us?

We *can* use various methods to intuit the major aspects of our life plan *at any given time* in our life, and to direct our conscious creation towards those areas. But there's also an alternative…

actively surrender to the universe

In the example above, when our efforts at conscious creation are being blocked by our higher self and guides, surrender would be far more appropriate than continued struggle against the tide. And this idea is found in many Eastern approaches.

Indeed sometimes with the benefit of hindsight we'll find we've reached a broadly similar outcome but via a completely unexpected route. As an example love might come to us via a wonderful new friend rather than the new partner we'd been aiming for.

For some this idea of surrender is rather more appealing than attempting to consciously create in line with a variety of shifting life goals that we can't be sure of anyway. Conscious creation requires that we trust sufficiently to eliminate fear. But surrender requires that we trust sufficiently to give up on trying to *control* everything.

So what does 'active' surrender mean?

For some the idea of surrender tends to have connotations of being somewhat passive – of just sitting back and letting the world revolve around us. And that's *not* what's being advocated here, which is why the word 'active' is so important to make the distinction explicit.

The first element of active surrender is that we fully accept we have a deliberate life plan, rather than regarding even this as illusory. The second is that we must be *brave* enough to totally trust the universe to carry us along this path. The third is that we must remain *open* to what the universe is trying to tell us and *flexible* enough to take its advice – as in not having fixed preconceptions about our path. This last is the one to which the word active most applies because we're always on the *alert* for messages coming via dreams, or via chance conversations or meetings, or via other synchronicities.

All this allows us to be easy on ourselves. Even though we're active we can also relax and let go. It allows us to flow with the universe far more effortlessly than any other approach.

So is conscious creation in conflict with active surrender?

No, we can do both. But everyone perceives the balancing of creation and surrender differently, so each of us must do whatever feels right for any given issue, or at any given stage in our life. The art is to recognize when to really push forward because everything is flowing nicely, and when to sit back, enjoy the journey and just see what unfolds. Pushing against a locked door is futile. Just wait until the universe turns the key for you.

Does active surrender still require us to do all the other work already discussed in this part?

Absolutely. For example we should still seek to develop self-love, meditate regularly and face up to our lower self. And as far as a positive approach to life is concerned, even when we're not consciously creating we'll still want to see life as a miracle, to be grateful for everything, and to see the good and the positive in all experiences.

If we actively surrender will everything be sweetness and light?

No. Our journey will be made up of experiences that are 'perfect' for us, but these will include some that are challenging, maybe even downright unsavory. This is exactly why even fully conscious creation cannot lead to a life with no challenges, because these will always be a part of our life plan however experienced we are.

When we face these challenges we *could* indulge in old, negative, fear-driven patterns of behavior – withdrawing, feeling sorry for ourselves, wondering 'why me?', allowing them to cast a shadow over our entire lives. But we also have a positive and love-driven alternative: 'Oh, how interesting, my soul must have chosen this experience and be growing from it.' We can then observe the emotions that come up with a little more detachment, safe in the knowledge that whatever we're going through has a higher purpose, and that everything is and will be fine.

If we've faced up to our lower self, and are bravely, openly and flexibly engaged in active surrender, we can be safe in the knowledge that the challenges we face will be minimized. They will only be those that are really helping us to grow. Of course our *human* impulse may still be to try to avoid them. But this would be a mistake because from the *soul* perspective, in terms of growth, they're the best bits of our life.

And that leads us neatly onto the final piece of advice, which is arguably *the* most important...

use your soul rather than human perspective

We've discussed the incredible complexity of the dynamics of our lives, and we've seen that often we don't really know what's happening under the surface for ourselves, let alone for other people.

Our earlier example was the motorist whose partner had just left him, but let's now take this a step further. Someone abuses a child. The obvious reaction is that they're a terrible, *evil* person. But the chances are that they were abused themselves as a child, and so on and so forth right back down the line. How accurate is our initial assessment now we know a little more about what lies beneath the surface?

Some people manage to break the cycle, which is fantastic, courageous and all the superlatives we can think of. But what about those who don't? Of course we have to take whatever steps we can to make sure they don't have access to children, so the temptation is removed, and to make sure they get help and counseling. But are they evil, or simply victims themselves?

Most people's outrage is provoked by the pain and anger we'd naturally feel if it happened to one of our children. But can we depersonalize it and rise above this obvious, fear-based reaction? It's not easy, but surely it's worth trying? Who benefits from just writing that person off as evil?

So what is our soul perspective, and how does it differ from our human outlook?

This whole book has been geared to bring us to this point, by helping us to think more deeply about who we are and how we feel about things. Hopefully together we've mastered the idea that we're responsible for our own destiny. Hopefully we've mastered the idea that we might choose a disability of some sort to accelerate our growth. Hopefully we've mastered the idea that we might lose a child as a test of our emotional reaction and maturity. We might even have managed to see that a pedophile can be a victim too.

All of this has been attempting to help us switch from our human to our soul perspective.

You might think that's as far as it goes, but it's not. There's an even more extreme test of our understanding, and you're going to be asked to push your boundaries one last time. We could of course shy away from this, and take the safe route, but if we were going to do that we wouldn't even have discussed pedophiles. And what follows is arguably one of the best ways to demonstrate the huge difference between the two perspectives. So here goes.

Was Hitler evil?

Please stop and think about everything you've learned so far before you jump straight in with outrage that this question might even be asked.

The answer is... almost certainly not. Think about it. WW2 dominated the course of tens of millions of lives right across the globe. Do we really imagine that such an event, with such an impact, could come about by pure chance? By one immature soul managing to come to power and wreak worldwide havoc?

In case you think this is really going out on a limb, a number of spiritual sources have talked in these terms before. And a number of regression subjects have recalled being war victims who knew exactly what they were volunteering for.

So if WW2 was planned, what was it all about? How could 'God' even allow such slaughter, let alone deliberately orchestrate it?

The answer is, as always, simple... to teach humanity a lesson.

It was meant to show us just how far from the ideal of unconditional love we were still capable of going in the twentieth century, for all our scientific and technological progress – in the hope it would teach us never to go there again. Of course you might argue that it didn't work, and that we're still fighting meaningless wars now – so what was, indeed is, the point of all this suffering?

Well, there's another, more love-based way of looking at the patterns of war that built to a crescendo of idiotic slaughter in the two worldwide conflicts of the last century. It's that arguably the scale of wars has decreased steadily since then, for all that more localized and sometimes hideously savage conflicts do still occur. And despite its terrible tragedies the new global threat of terrorism tends to produce far fewer casualties, so far at least.

So perhaps on a soul level the grand plan is working very well? Perhaps we can even suggest that all this conflict has played a major part in preparing the way for the global shift in consciousness we hear so much about? Realism is important but we always have the choice to see the glass as half-full or half-empty. Which do *you* prefer?

Of course you might still protest that we seem to be incredibly slow learners. But this brings us neatly onto another important aspect of soul perspective. As souls in the light realms we have no concept of time. It's merely a construct that we humans need in the physical plane to give us a frame of reference for our experiences.

So broadly speaking from a soul perspective we collectively don't *care* how many times we get it wrong. There's no rush. It's not a race. And one way or another we'll all get the experiences we need. It's mainly when we're in human form that we feel frustration at being such slow learners.

Then should we be unconcerned about man-made climate change for example?

Not at all. There can surely be little dispute that as humanity we should do everything in our power to protect and nurture our environment, and the animals and plants we share it with.

Are there any silver linings to the various crises' we're facing?

Yes. For example even if climate change were not man-made this whole process has forced us to think hard about our throwaway society, where everything is replaced instead of mended. About our ridiculous squandering of earth's reserves of fossil fuels, when we should be developing green and sustainable alternatives. And about our ludicrous focus on money, power and wars, when the whole carpet could literally be pulled from under our collective feet not too far from now.

Not only that, this is an issue that requires the whole human race to come together to take action, instead of continuing to indulge in petty rivalries.

Meanwhile there are some suggestions that the earthquakes, tsunamis and volcanoes of recent years have also played their part in helping to raise our consciousness. Perhaps the global outpourings of aid, compassion and love we've witnessed form part of the grand plan too?

So what is this global shift in consciousness?

The whole New Age movement was founded on the suggestion that as we entered the latter part of the twentieth century we were shifting from the astrological Age of Pisces into that of Aquarius. This was heralded as the dawn of a new era of love and peace.

More recently the focus has shifted onto various predictions concerning a major upheaval towards the end of the year 2012. And while this was originally perceived as something disastrous, increasingly it's being seen as the catalyst for a shift in humanity's collective consciousness. That is, a raising of our vibrations that'll connect us all more closely to our higher selves and to the light realms, along with myriad other spiritual developments.

What, then, does our future hold?

Humanity is indeed at a huge crossroads. On the one hand we seem to be staring into the abyss. On the other we're on the brink of a huge positive shift. Which one will come out on top?

Perhaps the prophecies of a huge catastrophe in the coming years are correct? After all there's evidence that a reasonably sophisticated global trading culture was almost entirely wiped out by a major comet impact tens of thousands of years ago, forcing it to rebuild from scratch. Perhaps it paid the price for forgetting its spiritual birthright?

Perhaps we've done the same, and the same catastrophic fate awaits? But would a significant decrease in population be so bad? After all, it would give the planet and her resources a sorely needed break. And if it happened suddenly, with another comet impact for example, it might be rather kinder than the lingering death tens or even hundreds of millions will face if the worst fears about irreversible global warming are right.

Above all it would allow humanity another fresh start. The chance to create a future in which the eventual reemergence of technology could be *allied to* a spiritual worldview, rather than overwhelming it with material preoccupations as it's done so far this time round.

In the meantime, with such restricted opportunities here on earth, many souls might move on to other planetary environments of different kinds to continue their growth. Perhaps this is one of the true meanings of the predictions of a huge shift in our consciousness?*

All this isn't meant to sound pessimistic. The aim is to inject some realism, and adopting a soul perspective at the right times can allow us a certain dispassionate distance from human cares and concerns.

So is it all doom and gloom then?

Absolutely not! We should still strive with might and main to achieve the positive outcomes from all these opportunities for change. We should assume we *can* save the earth without a massive catastrophe, and we *can* help to secure a more balanced place for humanity on its face.

That's why the efforts of ever increasing numbers of us are so vital. From those combating global warming, through to those clearing negative energies that have built up in certain parts of the planet. And from inspirational authors and speakers, through to individuals working quietly away at raising their own consciousness and that of those around them.

Every one of us is absolutely crucial to this process. *Every one of us* has a part to play. The smallest changes in what we do and what we think

---

* All these ideas are explored further in *The Future of the Soul* and *The History of the Soul.*

in our daily lives will have a much greater impact than we might assume. Please don't underestimate *your* power to change things.

We're increasingly coming together to try and make sure it's *our* generation, or the ones following closely in our footsteps, who'll create heaven on earth.

further reading

QUESTIONS

Lawton, Ian, *The Little Book of the Soul* (Rational Spirituality Press, 2007) and *The Big Book of the Soul* (Rational Spirituality Press, 2008).

SUGGESTIONS

These are just a select few of the self-help books that have had the most profound influence on me:

Beginners (these are all novels with a message):

Bach, Richard, *Illusions: The Adventures of a Reluctant Messiah* (Mandarin, 1992).

Coelho, Paulo, *The Alchemist* (HarperCollins, 1995).

Millman, Dan, *Way of the Peaceful Warrior* (H J Kramer, 1984).

Redfield, James, *The Celestine Prophecy* (Bantam, 1994).

Intermediate:

Ruiz, Don Miguel, *The Four Agreements* (Amber-Allen Publishing, 1997) and *The Mastery of Love* (Amber-Allen Publishing, 1999).

Stone, Sue, *Love Life, Live Life* (Little Brown, 2010).

Tolle, Eckhart, *The Power of Now* (Hodder & Stoughton, 2005).

Walsch, Neale Donald, *Conversations With God* (Hodder & Stoughton, 1997).

Advanced (the last two consist entirely of channeled material):

Aurobindo, Sri, *The Life Divine* (Lotus Press, 1990).

The Pathwork Lectures (for the full set of 258 lectures see www.pathwork.org, or for an introduction see www.ianlawton.com/se6.htm).

The Way of Mastery (Shanti Christo Foundation, 2005).

HUMANITY'S PAST AND FUTURE

Lawton, Ian, *The Future of the Soul* (Rational Spirituality Press, 2010) and *The History of the Soul* (Rational Spirituality Press, 2010).

the future of the soul
2012 & the global shift in consciousness

ian lawton
with janet treloar, hazel newton & tracey robins

the nature of our sources	6
the background to the current shift	7
the last shift	9
the shifts before that	17
souls moving on to other places	22
life on a more highly evolved earth	33
our ability to accelerate the process	42
why everything is as it should be	46
universal excitement over this unique opportunity	49

Although this book was always planned, its actual contents came about by one of those great synchronicities that those on a spiritual path learn to recognize and embrace.

It began on the evening of 4th March 2010 at Gaunts House, north of Wimborne, Dorset. I was a student attending a training module with the Past Life Regression Academy, run with a wonderful mixture of professionalism, integrity, spirituality and love by Andy Tomlinson and Hazel Newton. They always try to have some sort of evening activity or entertainment to help us unwind, because the days are pretty intense and high energy. Lots of personal issues come to the surface in our regressions, which is part of the learning process, but also ensures we've got rid of our own emotional baggage before we start acting as therapists to others.

On the first evening Hazel had agreed to guide one of the assistant trainers, Janet Treloar, into an altered state so that she could act as a channel for any energies from the light realms who might want to answer questions about 2012 and the global shift in consciousness. This is a technique not totally dissimilar to the one that Andy and I had used in *The Wisdom of the Soul*, although Janet is such an excellent trance subject that little induction is required. But it was hardly an exercise of the same rigor, because Hazel, myself and another assistant trainer, Tracey Robins, only had twenty minutes or so to prepare our questions. So we had no great confidence that they would yield significant results, and at the outset were really treating the whole thing as a bit of fun.

Yet as the session unfolded it became clear that we were witnessing something that was both powerful and important. Ever since she was small Janet has been open to the spirit world, but she soon learned to control and even repress this. She has never channeled on a regular basis, the previous time being about a year before during the same training module, but apparently even that had been very low key by comparison.

From the outset she began shaking from head to toe, and this continued throughout the hour-long session. Afterwards she said it felt like 'something about twenty feet long was trying to fit into my body', although half way through the first energy left and another even larger one came in. In fact as observers we all noticed a temporary respite in her shaking at this point.

What's more, not only was Janet showing channeling talents she hadn't fully tapped into before, but the messages coming through her were hugely positive and uplifting, yet still grounded. This is exactly what I'd been searching for, because the channeled offerings about 2012 and beyond I'd come across previously seemed to veer between doom-laden warnings of catastrophe on the one hand, and sugar-coated messages of spiritual ascension for 'the chosen ones' on the other. At the end of the session we all just looked at each other and said 'wow'!

We quickly realized that the wonderful messages we were being blessed with should be explored further and then delivered to a global audience as soon as possible. And the timing was surely no coincidence, given that I'd already been planning for my next book to be on exactly these topics. So I sorted the material into a number of main headings, and created a whole new set of detailed questions within each, designed to clarify and expand on the information we'd already received. Hazel and Tracey provided input to this process but Janet was deliberately left out.

The four of us met again for our second session on Easter Sunday, the 4th April, at Hazel's flat in Bristol. We were full of excitement and anticipation, sensing that the possibilities for gaining incredible insights and information were limited only by our own intellects and imagination. And as I put the questions to our sources over a lengthy session that lasted more than four hours, they didn't disappoint.

The major difference this time was that we were communicating with many more energies, and most of them tended to concentrate themselves in Janet's head area rather than entering her whole body. The exception was a small, rather excitable but totally delightful 'nature spirit' energy, who initially occupied her right shoulder but caused it to twitch so violently it was painful. When we had to ask him to calm down he moved into her legs, which in turn began to twitch, but thankfully less painfully.

To turn to the process itself, the quality of any channeled messages always depends not only on the wisdom of the source or sources themselves, of which more shortly, but also on the extent to which the human channel can 'get out of the way'. Indeed a 'clear channel' like Janet can remove themselves completely:

> I take myself off to my 'safe place', which is under an oak tree in a meadow. When I invite the highest sources available to literally step into me I give them permission to use my body and energy. So I try as much as possible to remain under that tree so my consciousness doesn't inhibit them using my mind and voice to process and convey the information they choose to share with us.

This method obviously works because, speaking from the experience of listening to the many, many hours of trance sessions conducted as research for *The Wisdom of the Soul*, there appears to be very little if any conscious interference in her transmissions. This is especially demonstrated by the delivery of her responses being relatively fast, with few hesitations. Indeed she was still flowing just as quickly and easily at the end of our four-hour second session as she did at the beginning.

Moreover virtually all the material received has been deemed useful and relevant, and therefore included in this book, with omissions mainly consisting of duplication between the two sessions. Admittedly I've often tweaked her spoken words to produce the transcriptions that follow, but this is only in terms of order, grammar, repetition and so on, to ensure they're as clear and concise as possible. Also the order of the first set of transmissions has been changed in places to fit into the major headings that were only developed subsequently. In each section the material from each session is presented in order to provide the best narrative flow for the reader. Occasionally explanatory notes have been added in square brackets.

As for the possibility that Janet was merely regurgitating previously acquired information, she has read some books about 2012, but much of what follows isn't found in or even contradicts their contents. In particular as far as historical information is concerned, she reports that she knows Jesus was born around 2000 years ago but very little from before that time – for example about earlier civilizations, or about global and human evolution in general.

In any case, by contrast to my normal approach to evidence under the banner of what I refer to as 'Rational Spirituality', this whole exercise was never designed to be rigorous and evidential. The sources we were working with weren't concerned with verifiable, low level information like 'what is my mother's name' or 'what was my grandfather's profession', although they probably could have got it if we'd pushed them. Indeed as you read through the interchanges you will see that we deliberately kept our questions at a relatively high level throughout, and didn't ask for undue detail. Some may see this as a weakness, but the reality is that the strongest message to come through was that the future of life on planet earth is by no means fixed. So it's pointless to ask detailed questions because the answer, if it's genuine and not consciously influenced, will tend to be 'it depends'.

In particular we didn't ask for details of exactly where future natural upheavals might occur. This is because, even if the information *was* accurate, it could only induce potential panic that would be entirely nonproductive – once you understand the proper spiritual context of such events, which will be explained in due course.

Despite its length, after our second session Janet was still semi 'tuned in'. And during these further discussions our sources did deliberate over whether they could give us details of a definitive event in the immediate future to prove their credibility. But because of the danger that free will might invalidate any prediction, we tended to see this more as a potential hindrance than a help. In fact she did receive a flash of some major political event in Russia, which we didn't pursue. Imagine our chagrin when exactly a week later the Polish president was killed in an air crash over Smolensk, and she knew this was exactly what they had been trying to show her.

Despite this we all still feel that the main thing with channeled material is to see if the information resonates with you, and if it does you just have to trust your sources. Of course you can ask them who they are. Indeed we did, and they said we could refer to them as 'the council', a large and fluid group that represents various aspects of our part of the universe. But such assurances of identity don't *prove* much, if anything, because if your sources are 'jokers in the pack' they're not going to admit as much, they're going to tell you that they're the 'masters of the universe' or some such.

Nevertheless, if you trust your sources we would suggest that it's preferable to be dealing with a group such as this, because they can bring in the relevant 'expert' to answer questions on a particular topic. By contrast single sources can have a more limited and sometimes biased perspective.

The one control we did think we could usefully employ was to send the draft manuscript to our friend and colleague Toni Winninger in the US, so that she could cross-check its contents with the 'Masters' that she has been successfully channeling for some years now. She kindly responded with support and a few items of clarification. But when we asked our own sources whether we should also follow what we understood to be normal protocol, that is reading back the final manuscript to them so they could check it for accuracy, their response was somewhat unexpected:

> We can give you information, but part of the process is that you resonate with it and put down what you feel will resonate with others. You will be able to judge that far better than us.

Indeed this is illustrative of the many apparently counterintuitive responses they gave us. They immediately felt more resonant than the response we might have expected, even though we are all fairly used to using our soul rather than human perspective. All of which – to us at least, and hopefully to you as well – lends a greater air of authenticity to these messages.

The four of us have found that the process of putting this book together has really accelerated our own energies. The more we've switched on to the possibilities of the shift, the more we've seen that the same expansive, positive attitudes found in the council's messages are actually everywhere we look. And we've realized just how many people really are waking up, and just how quickly. So on all levels we're hugely, hugely thankful to the various energies on the council for sharing their wonderful insights, and for allowing us to be involved in this process.

The next few years will contain much change and some hardship. But if these messages are right, and the four of us feel they most likely are, we should all be incredibly excited about an opportunity we've all been planning for and eagerly awaiting for literally thousands of years...

Ian Lawton
April 2010

the nature of our sources

SESSION 2

You have regularly used the term 'council' to describe yourselves. Can you tell us more about this?

It's a very human word. It just means a collective group of different consciousnesses that are from many different levels, places and species. It involves everything to do with earth, but also outside of earth as well, so the council is huge.

[The remaining information in this section was obtained from Janet when still 'tuned in' after our second session.]

How many souls are on the council?

A good few hundred, if not more because there are more in the background that come in at certain times. They are covering so many bases. There are lots of souls from other places and dimensions, and everything on earth is represented, the elemental kingdom, the human kingdom, the animal kingdom. Council is the term they use, but it's not a hard and fast thing, they bring different souls in for different things. They've learned this time so they bring in advice from new groups as and when they need it, for example to find out information 'on the ground' from people who have just left earth. There is a group from Haiti with the council now, and they are checking how the earth feels in these places.

What kind of souls are on the council?

Our part of the universe is like a cube that overlaps with others. The only soul we spoke to today who is involved with more than just our 'bit' was the 'helper of Source' [who talked to us about the last shift]. He actually dates back to the Big Bang and even the universe before that.

the background to the current shift

SESSION 2

What can you tell us about the shifts taking place on planet earth at this time?

All this has been going on for a long time. The shift started around a hundred years ago, but has really accelerated in the last ten years, and will culminate in the next seven. So while the majority of people will now actually see and feel the shift, it's been happening anyway, in the molecules throughout the body, shifting and changing throughout the generations, which is why you can now work consciously in this higher vibration. And the changes are not just across this planet but across many, many planets.

What will we actually experience?

The twitching you can see in her [Janet's] body is an intensified version of how the vibrations of the molecules will actually change and shift. But this will be a slower process than people think. People will just get naturally used to it, just become attuned to it.

Is that everybody?

In every living thing. It's working throughout and there'll be other things that people can see through this as it changes. Things that aren't clear at the moment to the naked eye will be. And the shift and change has to happen naturally for people to accept what they're seeing, and to believe what they're seeing.

SESSION 2

[The first energy we made contact with in the second session later revealed that they were heavily involved in the last shift.]

What proportion of the souls currently incarnated on earth are from other planets?

About an eighth.

How long have they been coming in for?

It's been increasing. It started sixty, seventy years ago. There's more now than there has been.

Is there anything else you would like to tell us about the background to the current shift?

Different cultures and different places have been awakened at different times. You live in a global world, technology has increased so you can take in what's happening all around the world at once. Things have had to change this time, one place cannot increase without the other, it's an amalgamation. And special attention was given to the West as it had not been awoken before, and it had to be done in a way that those people would accept. It was done more slowly and with a lot more difficulty than in other places.

Is this because it hadn't really happened here in the West before?

Minds were too set. There is a pack mentality that is not talked about. Those that were different were not necessarily accepted. But there were souls who chose that particular experimental route, and by speaking their truth many did battle against the tide. And it all helped, it just took longer than we expected. It's still not at the level it needs to be at now, which is why everything is increasing to such a degree.

So are things being accelerated now?

Yes. Extra help is being given, just like we are doing here with you. We've had to adapt to a mindset in the West that we weren't used to. Our help might not be in the way we would have originally chosen, but it is working. For example, we are aware of the way people worship 'celebrities' in the West, often more than they do religious or political figures, and we have used that to bring about much knowledge and awakening. Many celebrities are waking up other souls in their own right, through mediums that the West will accept.

So you've had to be flexible, but are you happy with the progress now being made?

Yes, we are happy. We are just surprised at how much we have had to adapt and change over the last few years, but it's all coming together now.

the last shift

SESSION 1

Has this happened before?

Yes, some 20,000 to 30,000 years ago in your terms.

What was the outcome then?

They didn't cope so well. Their bodies weren't as dense as they are now, and souls merged together and did things they really shouldn't. It was decided they should leave for a while, and have experiences in other places before coming back to earth. So many of them are trying this experience of an energy shift for a second time now.

And this time nothing is set in stone. That's the beauty of this experience, and why the whole galaxy is watching it. Never before has this been done, where the outcome is not certain.

SESSION 2

Can you tell us more about the last shift?

We are happy to talk about that, we have people that were there. It was a different time on earth, the goals were different. Souls wanted to learn about expansion. They already knew quite a lot, and they had the ability to change the form of their bodies as and when was needed. But they were learning about expansion outside of the body too, and even a removal of their energy out and then back in. Perhaps it happened too quickly. We thought they could cope better.

So did they have physical bodies?

Yes, but to different degrees. Some were denser than others. Those that could lead lives away from other souls could remain quite fluid in form, but the more they encountered other souls the more solid their form needed to be to remain separate. As long as they remained apart from the rest of society, even in groups that were on the same level, they knew how to keep themselves separate from each other. But, just like you see in cities now, when there is a closeness a natural soul energy exchange happens. And that can become very confusing once different personalities are in the mix, because some will naturally take and some will naturally give.

Previously you mentioned souls merging when they weren't supposed to. Is this what you're referring to now?

No, all this was before the energy shift. There was a difference between people already. We expected the expansion would be in those with more fluid bodies, but the dominant forms that emerged were those with the denser bodies. They were the ones that remained, and this is your lineage.

So could the denser people see the less physical people?

They could, but as the shift progressed it became more difficult for them. Those in the dense bodies used the increased energy to their own ends. Those with the more fluid bodies used the energy to leave, they didn't want to be a part of it. They had lived as part of a society together for a long time but the differences became too great, so they chose to leave.

Is there any similarity in the differences between the various types of people then and those that are emerging this time round?

Then you could see the differences with the naked eye, now you can't. That's why you need to see more with your heart than your eyes.

Why is it different this time round?

Last time we thought souls would come together even with their differences. That they would help each other, and enjoy the expansion together and use it wisely. This time there is a far greater capacity to help one another, to help those who aren't seeing to see. The memories of before are in all our souls. They are very deep and no one wants what happened before to happen again this time.

When did all this happen?

It's part of the 26,000 year cycle that is easy to find reference to in your culture now. [This is discussed more in the next section.]

Whereabouts was the human population concentrated on the earth 26,000 years ago?

Near the equator. The way the earth was then the climate had more extremes, and human life was most comfortable nearer the equator. Nearer to the poles there was very little life at all. The most evolved souls were right on top of the equator.

Can you give us an idea of the level of culture they had in those days? What was their most sophisticated technology, for example?

Their technology utilized the power of their minds. Some created purely with their minds, but almost had to dedicate their whole lives to doing this, and to separating themselves off. But more and more these people used what the earth had given them to create, and they involved their minds more, a skill which has since been forgotten.

Can you explain what you mean by 'create'? Create what?

Create comfortable places to live. Create sources of sustenance, food and drink.

Do you mean they could literally create a building or some food from nothing?

They could find sources of water, for example, and they knew how to adapt them to their bodies just by thinking. So if there was an impurity within the water they would be able to find out and remove it with their minds. And the same with food. They could help their crops grow, but they still used the land. There were those that could, as you would think, create something out of thin air, but a lot of energy was put into that. So other methods were used, crystals especially.

How were they used?

Again with the power of the mind, by linking with a crystal they would find its special purpose and adapt to the world around them rather than trying to get the world to adapt to their will. This is how they had progressed up until the shift, by understanding this.

So prior to the shift they were living in harmony with the earth and with nature?

Very much so. They loved beauty. Their culture was the arts. Their colors were so vivid.

They clearly lived in permanent settlements, but did they have cities as we would think of them now?

Yes. Many came together with the idea that they would learn. Their schools taught them how to harness the power of their thoughts, and those highest in the field of technology went out trying to find different ways to apply it. But as more people came together the more they also realized how they could use the power of each others' minds. There was a new surge of energy coming through from the earth, and as energy doesn't have a consciousness itself people could use it for whatever they wanted, including for their own ends.

With their minds they could send others mad. There was physical violence. But the worst were those who understood and were adept at what they could do, and who harnessed their energies together like a battery. They got into other people's minds, and would use their energy too. This was a complete mutation of their abilities, and not what was meant at all. It wasn't right, it wasn't the way that minds should work, but once made it was hard to break their contact with others' minds.

Was this all as a result of them having free will?

Yes they had free will, but they also didn't have a soul plan as you do now. Their life purpose was left up to them to decide during their incarnation. This was also changed after this time. We learned that within an incarnate body it is very hard even for a very evolved soul to truly remember about spirit and so on if beforehand they don't have a plan set in place to do so. There is a baseness associated with the earth, and that baseness can draw souls who are power-crazed.

All around the globe we have ancient traditions and sacred texts that talk about a 'Golden Age' and how it collapsed into decadence. Presumably this is what you are describing for us now?

Yes. Hedonism, power struggles and violence ensued. It was meant that signs would be left, that could be rediscovered at a time when this could happen again. This is the imprint, it is a memory imprinted on all our souls of what not to do.

What happened to end this previous civilization, was there some sort of upheaval?

I was part of the council back then. We discussed with those that oversee the earth how best to stop this. The earth was aware that it had its own power whereby it could grant great fertility, but it could also wreak much havoc. A contract was struck. Myself and others did not want to know exactly what would happen as we had chosen to incarnate at that time, to help to take many souls away into the light as it ended.

So many of us were needed to make sure that those who needed to move on were moved away from the edge of the energy as the ripple effect moved out into the surrounding spaces. We knew something would happen naturally. Where I was a wall of water as high as a mountain hit us. Then many of us hovered above the scene as we watched what happened below, before we took those souls we needed to with us. And the earth shook and shook, and eventually the water took what it needed to and cleansed it. Everything came from water first, so everything went back. It was right of the earth to do it this way.

So it was an earth thing, not the impact of a comet or anything like that?

Not *that* time.

Perhaps I can ask you about yourself. Are you one of the entities we talked to last time?

No. I have been brought in to speak at this time because I was present during the last shift. It was the last time I incarnated on earth.

You mentioned that you were on the 'council' back then too, perhaps you can tell us a little more about that?

There were many of us from different parts of the universe. We tried to combine our ideas, things that had worked in other places. But duality on the earth is within everything that lives on it, so those things that had worked in other places didn't necessarily work here. People were drawn too much to extremes to appreciate them. You could say I was the centre of the council. I had also come from somewhere else, but I understood earth.

I was all for the project, and I was one of those who brought in these souls from elsewhere with their own experiences. I expected the level of soul advancement on earth to be such that they would succeed. There were many of us, so it wasn't just my decision, but I shouldered the responsibility with the others when it did not go according to plan. And afterwards I pledged to help the next time around.

What proportion of the human population was wiped out by this upheaval?

Only about forty percent. Those that remained were in places where the land was not so fertile, but also the energy was not so strong and they had not been so corrupted.

What size of population did the earth have then?

Not even one percent of what we have now.

Is this former civilization what some people would refer to as 'Atlantis'?

It is. Not that we called it that, but the word itself has a resonance that energetically awakens those who were involved at the time to a memory, an imprint. We hope this means that when they feel the new energy now it will not be corrupted again. It is an important word.

Because of its resonance?

When people say it they are filled with hope and optimism.

New beginnings?

Yes.

Have a lot of the souls that were there during the last shift returned to experience this one?

Yes. Although most have been having experiences in other places in the meantime, many of them were horrified with what they had done, and have been determined to make sure that if they experienced it again they would not be corrupted.

You see these people more in certain parts of the world. There are those in the East who are already able to manipulate energy to change certain things. You may have read about them, for example monks in the Himalayas, and Tibet in particular, which resonates completely with Atlantis. And souls that had very fluid form last time have tended to select these types of lives now, for this change, so they can again be partly removed from society and go back into those memories of how to change and shift energy.

You suggested in the last session that the outcome was known last time round, whereas this time it's not. Can you explain how that works given what you've just told us?

Those above me, for want of a better word, did know that this experiment of bringing in energy to a place of duality, and trying things that had worked in other places, would not work. They knew that we had much to learn about the soul, and how much it could remember while still functioning within the human form. But we needed to learn this. Perhaps that's why this is still so painful to me, because I believed so truly that it would work. But you're right, they did know that this experiment wouldn't work, at that level it was always known. Yet we learned so much from it that, even though I and others felt it was a failure at the time, subsequently there was a massive leap in evolution as a result of what was learned.

Is it not the case that nothing is ever a failure because it is all experience?

It was a failure in my eyes because of the part I played, but overall it wasn't. The earth itself discovered that it could focus its attention as well. Up until that point it had never been asked to focus its attention within itself to actually change the forces around it and make something happen in a specific place. So it too was discovering about itself.

Can we return to the issue of when this last upheaval happened?

26,000 years ago. The earth used the surge of energy to be able to do these things.

There appears to be physical evidence on the earth that there was a major comet impact about 11,500 years ago, which would have decimated the global population. Is that something you could confirm?

It wasn't something I was involved in.

Perhaps we could ask whoever can answer that question to step forward?

[This new energy later identified themselves as a 'helper of Source'. Janet noted subsequently that it felt somewhat remote and aloof.]

There was involvement across the universe, and the earth was impacted just like a number of other places. This was going to happen and therefore the earth used it as a time of purification. The weather systems would change so that it would be encased. So while there was an encasement on the outside, much energy could be stored and nourished within. It knew it was preparing for a time when there would be many things living on its back. So it was a way to prepare for such a time. It was basically taking advantage of an event that was going to happen, and affect other parts of the universe, anyway.

Do you mean that it absorbed the energy of the impact itself and was able to store it in some way?

The energy was taken inside, and the casing on the outside gave it time to infuse this energy into every particle on the earth before it could be lost to the atmosphere. There is always much energy stored within the earth that is let out as and when it's needed.

So the earth itself had a major cleansing 26,000 years ago, and then there was another major episode as a result of the comet impact 11,500 years ago?

The change 26,000 years ago actually made the earth more fertile throughout, so although it reduced the human population significantly it had less impact on the earth itself. 11,500 years ago was a dramatic change for the earth, preparing it for the situation we're now in with so many souls on its face.

But presumably a significant proportion of the human population was wiped out 11,500 years ago as well?

They were, but population had dwindled anyway because we knew this was going to happen. Many souls chose not to incarnate at that time and just to watch, or they continued their journey in other places. Not so many people were wiped out then as is commonly thought because less people were on the planet.

Perhaps I can just ask you about yourself. Are you on the council that looks after the earth?

Shall we say I am an advisor to a number of different places. It's best for me not to say exactly where I am from at this time, except that I can answer this: I was part of the process that impacted the earth at that time. There was a wider picture involved, it was something that had to happen. I am a 'helper of source'. I do not have a name that you would understand.

the shifts before that

SESSION 2

To go right back to the fundamentals, do universes get created one after the other, and does each one somehow become more refined?

More or less. Each one concentrates on different qualities, different things it has learned from the universe before. The universe we are in now is discovering the full range of the physical. No universe before has been so solid.

So there is a sense of building on and learning from what went before?

Absolutely. The consciousness remains. Some universes previously were not much different from each other, but this one is very different.

To return to the 26,000 year cycle, has this had an impact on life on earth from the outset?

Since the earth came into existence it has had an impact, because since that time there have been the beginnings of living organisms. Anything that lives on the earth goes through the earth's shifts and changes with it, so these are displayed or at least mirrored in each organism's energy field.

It goes right back to the beginning and the sea. The seas and the oceans were always the breeding grounds, the experimental laboratories. It took many, many years for the right types of organisms to start coming through that could have a consciousness within them.

Was this being directed in any way?

You would call it the 'hand of God'. There had to be a lot of direction from other places, lots and lots of different places that already had lifeforms came together to create something new, something different. It took longer than was expected as this was always going to be a place of duality, and that hadn't been experienced before. For things to be set up properly it all had to be perfect, the perfect surroundings, otherwise it was all just going to die out again, and nobody wanted that. So there was a lot of direction initially, before we could sit back and see what would happen once soul consciousness took over and did what it wanted with those bodies.

The earliest human forms appeared a couple of million years ago. Were there any problems with sophisticated soul energy trying to work with bodies and brains that weren't particularly advanced?

No, because the soul energies coming in were relatively inexperienced and not very aware of their own potential at that time. Everything went at its own pace while physical form evolved and became more sophisticated. The very earliest consciousnesses that went into human form were brand new. They needed what you would now consider to be very, very simple lives. Emotions hadn't been brought in, and many other attributes that you would now consider to be associated with a human soul were not there. The first thing they had to master was survival. Without learning about a need to survive, progression could not have happened, and this had to be achieved before they could bring anything else in. You would not recognize their energy as a human energy now.

How long have what we would refer to as 'modern humans' been on the planet?

It's hard to answer as the level of consciousness and the level of energy body are different things, and we have experimented with many different combinations over the course of human history. You have been as you are now for approximately 5000 years.

Ok, to put it another way, when did reasonably advanced soul forms first start to be able to incarnate on planet earth in some sort of a human-like body?

75,000 years ago.

Does that mean there was a major step forwards at this time in terms of the sophistication of the soul energy and the physical body?

That's the time that, if you encountered that soul energy now, you would understand it as human. Earlier than that you would not.

Is the date of 75,000 years meant to represent three cycles ago?

Yes.

On a more general note, have highly evolved souls incarnated at various times in human history to assist the development of human culture?

It's happening the whole time. Humans come into the world with amnesia, so from a very early age they rely on and look to others for knowledge. So self-discovery and growth needs to be encouraged by those who are more 'evolved' as you would say, or as we see it those whose purpose is for the whole not the one. They choose to remember more, to instinctively 'know' from soul, and feel compelled to share this with others.

Many religious icons throughout the world have been on this path, in fact all the main ones in every religion. Each shared their knowledge at appropriate times to introduce great change, and the energy of these learnings is what remains. And religion is only one vehicle. Progression is inevitable, and wisdom is not exclusive to religion, the opposite in fact. You'll find it in the inspirational souls who have been leading lights in, for example, science, literature, art, music, health and politics – those who have tapped into a part of themselves that connects us with everything, and then used it to bring new and inspired knowledge through. You can see it now in popular culture, in those who have overcome adversity, illness or disability and then shared their inspired learnings with others.

Highly evolved souls often incarnate in the unlikeliest of bodies, in which they are not seen as glamorous or alluring by the masses. They work alone or in small groups to change the course of history, introducing progressive change in difficult times. This has always been the way, from the time when souls first chose amnesia.

Presumably by 'amnesia' you mean that once incarnate we don't consciously remember that we are soul energies whose real home is in the light realms. But when did souls first choose to have this amnesia?

Towards the end of the Golden Age, shortly before the last shift, humans were progressing well. The bodies of those who are your ancestors today had evolved fully into the now recognizable human form, and life was thriving. Initially amnesia was just an experiment, not all chose it. Those who felt they would learn more with amnesia were the pioneers, but their fate was to be an unknown without their memories from before. They would either succeed in integrating and learning from society, or they would become outcasts due to their 'baseness'.

When souls returned home they found they had learned much from this, especially the difficult experiences, so it wasn't long before all souls chose this route. But then many of them started to take the wrong path, and instead of creating they became destructive.

Ah, so it was the amnesia experiment that caused the havoc just before the last shift. What happened before souls had amnesia?

Before this, when souls incarnated in human form they brought with them the group memories of the human race, much as most animals still do now. This was the only way they could survive and still evolve.

So what happened after the last shift, when the amnesia experiment went wrong?

Souls continued to reincarnate with amnesia, but we had to change the rules, so we introduced the idea of individual life plans and triggers to help people remember what they were supposed to be doing. And that was much more of a success, indeed it is how you still operate today.

Did anything important happen during previous energy shifts in the 26,000 year cycle?

Around 75,000 years ago there was a major upheaval that caused a bottleneck in human evolution [this must be a reference to the well documented Toba super-eruption]. So souls from elsewhere decided to use that energy shift to introduce some major changes. They chose one strain of surviving human, and they continued to influence the evolution of their physical bodies to improve their chances of survival, although by influence we mean energetically and not by physical, genetic experiments as some of you seem to believe. From that point on all the other strains, including the Neanderthals, started to die out, even if it took some time for them to become completely extinct. It is no coincidence that the evidence of these extinct human forms has been unearthed in the last hundred and fifty years, in order that in the run up to the current shift we would be able to reveal what was really going on from a soul perspective.

In the next shift, around 50,000 years ago, there was no major upheaval. But because by then humans had properly mastered basic survival, the emphasis switched from influencing physical development to influencing emotional development. Then culture could progress much faster and people could come together to live in larger, more settled communities. Also over time humans started to have longer life spans and more individualized soul memories, and this is what developed into the Golden Age before the last shift.

Do we always have help from souls from other places during these shifts?

Yes, because the shift of 75,000 years ago was such a resounding success, and these souls can bring in ideas that have been tried in different environments. But progression happens within the cycles too, there are constant developments and evolution taking place. Then it's as if a new surge of energy comes through to feed the next 26,000 years. And so the cycle of growth, progression, experience and expansion continues.

So does this cycle represent an uplifting of earth's energy vibrations each time?

It's two steps forward, one step back. It's always increasing, but it gets very depleted in that time, so the surge has to take into account what's been depleted and then add more besides.

So the current shift is just another part of this cycle, but it's becoming progressively more sophisticated and the energy levels are going up all the time?

They are. The difference is also in the number of consciousnesses present, not just human but animal. And you have very many spiritual consciousnesses without physical form that inhabit the earth too. This hasn't been done before, which is why this shift is quite different.

So what causes the 26,000 year cycle?

The universe is set up in such a way that variations within it will prevent it from becoming stagnant, there will always be scope for change to varying degrees. The universe is a masterpiece of design, architecturally complex even when viewed from the perspective of the dimension you reside in. Through science and mathematics you've discovered some of the rudimentary forces governing your solar system, and indeed the universe, and you begin to understand its nature. It is architecturally perfect for its purpose, which is to constantly change and evolve. The constant and infinite alignments being made throughout direct energy, which then propels and activates change, so everything is constantly moving forward.

Of these infinite alignments the one that affects the earth every 26,000 years has a specific purpose. It was set up to influence more than just your planet, but due to its magnetic nature the earth isn't just part of the alignment, it's central to it. Its movement to a slightly different position ensures it is in direct alignment to receive energy from many other parts of the universe, and indeed dimensions too. And it is magnetically weak enough that it has a greater capacity for change to take place.

You'll find reference to this cycle in the calendars, astronomical predictions and sacred geometry of your historical civilizations, to guide the way for future generations and to give them something to aspire to.

The wobble of the earth's polar axis, which we refer to as 'precession', has a 25,920 year cycle. Does that have anything to do with all this?

Yes. Nothing on this scale happens by chance, and this apparent 'imperfection' was deliberately created and designed so that earth's alignments with other parts of the universe would constantly change. This technique is used elsewhere too.

souls moving on to other places

SESSION 1

Can you explain about parallel universes? Is this something we will experience as a result of this change?

That's where some people will leap. There is another place just like this. You won't find it as you look out of your telescopes towards the universe, it's set up in another place in another time. And those that find the correct route will find it.

Is there only one 'other place'?

There's the question. The answer's infinite. As the raising of the vibration happens you'll see what you want to see. It's a similar experience to what you call death. Your reality afterwards is what you want it to be. All the realities are out there, it's what you decide to see, and you'll be taken there.

Much has been said about the actual dates in December 2012. What relevance do these dates have for this energetic shift?

It's about the celestial connection. The alignments. Everything in place. Think of it as a super highway. If many souls are going to go to different places that they haven't been before, they have to have a vehicle to help them there. It doesn't mean this is a set time and place because things change day by day. But this is a date to work towards, and for souls to start to awaken consciously to the awareness of what might be happening, so they follow the path when they get there.

Can you explain that a little more clearly in the sense of what these people might actually experience?

It's like following a path, an energy path beneath your feet on the earth, like ley lines, but these are paths set up in the heavens. Not everyone will be doing this, but there are certain pockets of souls that will be going to other places, and they'll feel a pulling from their heart to these places. So it's the same thing, it's like following the energy beneath your feet, but this is high above, and so it's a helping hand, a guide to take them to the relevant place.

So much of the universe has to be involved because we couldn't do this without the help of energies from the other places they're going to.

The leap will actually shift them into a different place. And they're not just leaving the earth, they're leaving what you call 'home' too. And so many going together will see a leap that has not been seen for so long. It should be a time of rejoicing. The earth is growing, as are all the souls on it.

So does that mean their physical body will die at this time?

Well their energy will go, so yes.

Do we have a percentage of the population that has chosen to do this?

It's a minority.

So is all this almost a bit of an experiment for you too?

Completely. This is why so many souls have wanted to come from other places. There is no fear when they come though, everyone knows their soul survives, and they take their chances.

SESSION 2

[At this point in the second session, having established that we needed to talk to a different energy about this topic, the new energy revealed that they were the first of the two we spoke to in the first session.]

Last time you mentioned souls using the energy shift to propel them to other places. Can you tell us more about that?

There are a number of other places that are similar but not the same as the experience on earth. Places where souls experience emotions, for example. Many of those places have been set up alongside earth for eons, such as Sirius, and now they have opened the door to many more souls coming in, and this is an ideal time to do this.

There are also other places that are in other dimensions, and this is another shift, you might even refer to it as in a different time as well as a different space. If you could see all this it would look like a grid, it's almost like setting coordinates, just as now if you were planning a journey on earth you would use coordinates. The knowledge will be within to help people. It's another way of souls having their coordinates set to a new destination so that they can get there quickly.

What kind of bodies exist in other places that are physical? Is there anything like human form elsewhere?

In some places the bodies are very similar indeed. In others it's more as if the consciousness exists without a body. Individuality still stands strongly, and there are experiences to be learned from in these places, but a physical body is not needed.

Do these latter experiences occur in physical or nonphysical environments?

All possibilities exist.

What proportion of the souls going on to other places have spent most of their incarnations on earth, rather than coming from other places?

It was agreed that this 26,000 year cycle would be a good time for change, as many councils had met due to earth souls requesting other experiences. Many had now experienced most of the things they could or wanted to on earth. So this was a good time to utilize the shift to take them to other places, and the majority that are doing this are those who have had predominantly human experiences to this point.

In the last session you mentioned that only a minority of the human population would be going off to these other places, but can you now give us a percentage?

Fifteen to twenty percent perhaps. It's a minority, but with the amount of people on earth at this time it's still a very large number, which hasn't happened before. You will have witnessed this already. Never before have so many people led such extreme lives. Never before has there been such a need for therapists such as yourselves. When many souls who had not considered such a change before heard this was happening they decided to speed up the rest of their earth experiences, perhaps taking on three or four times what they might have worked through in previous incarnations, because they too wanted to go on this journey.

Some are going as soul groups as well. And because there will always be some that are more advanced in the group than others, they are helping each other to make the changes they need to. So there is much activity on the earth at this time, which can make it quite uncomfortable for those who aren't going through that experience.

So the increase in therapy and so on is all to help people to work through far more than they normally would?

Very much so. Many expressed a wish to complete their unresolved issues prior to the energetic shift so they would be able to appreciate and accept it fully. The help given speeds up this process.

Can you explain how incarnating on earth helps souls to go to other places?

While you are incarnate you can experience extremes that you cannot experience without a physical form. While you are immersed in love in your spiritual home you do not push yourself to extremes. The survival instinct that is within all of you when incarnate, and is your most base quality, drives these extremes. But when you are at an extreme level, a new surge of energy coming through can create new possibilities. That is why this can be used as a vehicle to attain these other places, whereas souls immersed in love might not be at the frequency level that is most appropriate to take in this energy to make the leap. It's not necessary but it is a help.

And unlike the negative 'battery effect' that arose during the last shift, this time it will be used in a positive way by many, many souls, so that those who are struggling will be taken along by the others, and those who are stronger will take the weak with them. It will be a time when souls merge, but in the correct way, without corruption.

And this merging will take place only when they are no longer in physical form?

Yes, and only for a short time.

So this isn't the only way to attain these other places?

They could do it while in nonphysical form, indeed some are doing just that. But they are missing out on an experience that only comes round once every 26,000 years. So many have simply chosen to do this because it's an adrenalin rush, as you would call it, like nothing else.

Are these other places also going through shifts in their own right?

Most are stable now. A few aren't fully stable, but only those souls who are prepared for the next stage to be an unknown quantity will be going to them. Most will be going to places where there will be stability and a rest really. A rest for their energy while it stabilizes and gets used to these new places. And they will be changing frequency too.

And most of these souls have never experienced places like these before?

That's correct.

Do these souls all have contracts to go to specific other places, is that already decided?

Most have decided within their groups, and will travel in their groups. These may not be their primary groups, but they are the ones they are in for this shift.

How many of these other places are there?

If you could see the grid it would look like a maze. There are so many different places, but the choices are limited because there might be a similar experience to be had in any number of them. Overseers will have decided where the most appropriate place is for each soul. Some are choosing a break, and others are choosing a more challenging role.

You said just now that souls can experience emotions in some of these other places, so does that mean they have full duality like the earth?

None have the duality that earth has, they tend to be more gentle emotional environments. For many it will be a familiar thing to still have emotions, this will help them through this time of change. But they will only be emotions that we would describe as comfortable and happy.

So earth really is unique in terms of its duality?

In this part of the universe, in this dimension, yes.

Can you explain? Do you mean there are other physical parts of the universe that have environments similar to that of earth?

The universe is immense, and there are those that oversee different parts. There are other councils, and if it is happening here there is no doubt it will be happening in other parts as well. But in terms of the part we deal with there is only a place for one such environment with duality.

What about the dimension issue?

It's to do with vibration and frequency. There are other dimensions where everything has a slightly different vibration and frequency, so they would look and feel much the same as the one you're in now, but be slightly different. A slight change can change the perception and experience of a place significantly, and again there are councils that are in tune with that.

Does that mean there are other places very much like earth, just on a different vibrational frequency?

Yes.

Some people think there are an infinite number of replicas of the physical earth, where the experience is only minutely different between each one. Can you comment on whether or not that is correct?

It is to a degree. There are other places within the universe that are playing out similar stories as it were, and if there is a benefit to your soul experience you can go to these other places without taking your physical form. There is a way to step between these dimensions at the same time, and some people know how to do this while still incarnate.

To clarify, some people suggest that if I move my left little finger a little bit, for example, that creates one reality, and then there is another one created at the same time in which it is my right little finger that moves. Do new parallel realities get created every time even the slightest decision is made?

That's not the way we perceive it. It's not as straightforward as that. It's more about the thought processes that are going on, and the group reality that is being created.

So as souls we come together to create group experiences, we don't do it individually?

It is as a group, that's correct.

You mentioned Sirius as one of the other places, is that a physical experience?

Yes.

Does it have human-type life forms on it?

It would feel familiar for a human soul to be in that body, and many of the souls going there have had experiences there already, before coming to earth. So even though they have led the majority of their lives on earth, many have happy memories of Sirius and they will gladly return there. Souls who want a more peaceful next incarnation are going there.

Are there any other planets in our solar system that play host to soul experience, even if it's not as part of a physical existence?

There has been an investigation of possibilities on each and every one of the planets in our solar system. This is why we are drawn to explore those planets. It's why some souls still believe we could exist on some of those planets. Unfortunately for them the memory is still very strong of a time when we possibly could have generated some sort of life form on those planets. None would support life as they are now, but there is a memory. The solar system is like a family, these are all siblings and there is a connection between them.

So there was a time when the other planets in the solar system could have supported life?

Not life as you perceive it, but there were consciousnesses that worked within each to see if some form of life that could hold consciousness could be created on them.

Did that ever happen on any of them?

There is a substance like water on Mars, and there have been similar experiments there to the one when we first started experimenting with the earliest life forms in the water on earth.

But there wasn't advanced life on Mars a long time before earth?

No.

Apart from Sirius are there any other stars that we would recognize where souls will be going during the shift?

You have telescopes now that can see the birth of stars, and some souls will be moving on to help with developing these new star systems. It's a slightly different consciousness, they will be using their experience of creation from the previous civilization, and of being part of what you might consider a blending of soul consciousness, to achieve this. But although they will connect with other souls there will still be strong individuality, so only those souls that have a strong sense of self have been allowed to take on such a mission. And we call it a mission because it is such.

At the birth of a new star system it is incredibly important that consciousness goes in to oversee the new creation within it, and only those who will stay true to the mission and not introduce their own agenda are selected. But these places can be seen on your telescopes, they're not that far away.

In the last session you mentioned a 'super highway'...

We prefer the term 'grid'.

Ok, you said that souls will be using this grid to attain other places via some sort of celestial alignment in 2012. But you also said there is no definitive date for this shift because it changes from day to day. How can both of these things be true?

This grid is immense and goes in many different directions, and as the celestial alignments change the access to these other places on the grid opens up. So the date that is talked of is like a lynchpin in all of this, but it is not the only one, it is just one alignment and one that can be seen with your telescopes. There is a lesser one in November 2011 that will be noticeable, then the main ones will be approximately a year apart. It will be as if there is a crescendo, with different things happening at different times, but roughly a year apart up to 2015.

So about five major alignments?

There could be as many as seven, depending on what happens. Seven is the number of completion. As always things may need to be adapted.

And everything will be completed by 2015?

In respect of souls who are moving on, yes, but the full changes and adaptation on earth will take longer. In 2015 the energy in the grid will be reversed back into the earth to help those that are struggling with the adjustment and the frequency change, so they may feel a resurgence that is simply this energy coming back into the earth.

When each alignment occurs, is it a physical alignment to the places they are going to?

It's more that you would look at the gaps where they have a clear path without the pull of other planets and stars in the way, ones that you might not be able to detect. Electromagnetism comes into play here, this is a way for them to go without being pulled to places they shouldn't go to.

So the alignments are all about getting the gaps right?

Exactly.

Will there be other souls acting as guides to help these souls as they journey across the grid?

Yes, there are many waiting. Many have come from the places they are traveling to. Many are even waiting as we speak, and have chosen not to take on anything else until this time has passed. There will always be some souls who will leave before their due date as well, so guides will be waiting for them to make sure they go to the correct places.

So if there are only between five and seven major alignments, does that mean there are only this number of places souls are going to?

The alignment simply means there is space for them to go, but each time they will be going out in many directions to many different places.

On a similar tack, if there are between five and seven major alignments, does that mean we are looking for the same number of physical events in which their lives will be taken?

It is likely that these will be times when the majority of the souls involved will leave in what you would describe as natural upheavals.

Are these going to be spread all around the globe?

Yes, there will be nowhere that is untouched by this.

We have had some major upheavals already, for example the tsunami in Indonesia. Was that the beginning of this process?

That was more in the way of preparation. Many of those souls are already incarnate again now but in a new, more evolved, energy body. And there are children who will come of age as the shifts happen who will be comfortable with the new energies, and they will become the new leaders, although this will be more in an advisory than in a leadership role as we know it at present. They will find that people gravitate to them to make it more comfortable for themselves. They may be leaders or advisors within communities or within whole countries.

So the major upheavals so far have not been of the same type as the ones to come?

They are necessary in that the earth is like a huge muscle flexing itself, getting ready for what it needs to do, and as this happens there will naturally be what you would call upheavals. And because the earth is so populated there is nowhere this can happen without many souls being a part of it, so they have already agreed to this. They are not so much going to other places though, it's just that this was their time and they had agreed to help the earth.

In terms of future upheavals, are there any major ones planned for this year, 2010?

There will be three more this year related to preparation for the energetic shift.

Is this also the start of souls going to other places?

The vibrational energy is changing, but it's only just starting to change noticeably in people's physical bodies, so not many people are choosing to leave for other places yet as part of their original plan. Some are getting ready to help others in the next series of events. They are more at what you would call guide level.

Will all the people who get caught up in the upheavals from 2011 onwards be going to other places?

No. There will be many where it is just their time to leave this incarnation as normal. But more generally the reason this process works both for the earth and for the souls involved, though it may sound distasteful while still in a human body, is that the adrenalin and fear felt just before the event will help to propel their energy as a group, and remind them all to go as one. It's not that suffering is needed, but this extreme emotion at the point of death in a large group of people will be needed, or at least appropriate, for the major leaps to other places.

Please remember also that this has been agreed, they know what is going to happen and they know that any suffering will be momentary, relatively speaking. As soon as they leave their bodies it will be different, they will feel that pull, they will feel the coordinates kick in. They will not have the same choices as normal, that is to stay and think and ponder what's just happened. It will be too quick. By the time they think of that they will be halfway to their destination.

We hear many people talking about a 'pole shift'. Is this likely?

That is happening, it's one of the things the earth is processing. The weakening of the magnetic field will actually help the souls going to other places.

Does this mean big climate changes?

Relatively speaking the magnetic field does not affect climate as much as it may affect many species of animal, particularly those living in the sea. It will be confusing because their coordinates will not work any more. But it is a time of evolution for them as well, and the strongest will survive.

In the last session you mentioned that some of the people going to other places are shifting their 'home' too. Can you clarify this?

The home we are referring to is the place that soul consciousness goes to between lives. It's a place where you have no physical body and your frequency is different. It's also where you can connect with your higher self to enable all your soul memories to come through, and where you can be an active part of Source as a whole. But each dimension shall we say has its own home. Some other places are in a different dimension or vibration, so their home is different too, even though it will still feel familiar.

Would it be best to think of these different 'homes' just as different vibrational aspects of the one home rather than as different 'places'?

Yes.

Is there anything else you think we need to know about souls moving on to other places?

Only that the actual experience of leaving will feel like a 'pulling'. A very quick, rapid pulling that comes from the heart centre. This is how we've decided to do it this time, to take the mind out of the equation. We don't want to take free will away, but we also expect that there would be a lot for these souls to contend with if they had the normal thought processes immediately after death.

We have an assumption that a soul will experience pretty much what it expects to after death, at least initially. Is this normally correct?

Yes. Normally what they experience is their own reality, although it is influenced by their guides helping them to project whatever they want. But in the current special circumstances there will be guides around who will be helping with the energy coming from the heart, and almost shielding the mind from any confusion until a later time when they can safely go through that. So the experience isn't being taken away, it's just being saved til a slightly later time.

All of this is clearly going to result in a significant reduction in global population levels. Can you give us an idea of the most likely percentage reduction?

Approximately twenty-five percent.

But presumably there is some flexibility around that because of free will?

It could be as much as forty percent if violence breaks out again. We can estimate approximately how many people will ignore and block the change, those who will find it more and more difficult and resort to violence. But we have estimated it as quite a low number, and perhaps that reflects our optimism that this time humans will tune into their souls more. However if more struggle and resist and there is more violence, that may taint those who have opened up and they may revert back as their survival instinct kicks in. Remember this was the first instinct instilled, and under pressure it will always override all others.

We haven't really discussed what we refer to as 'global warming', but one of the things predicted is that large parts of the globe will suffer severe water shortages. Is that your understanding too?

Once the shift has occurred and the population has been reduced, the earth has a great capacity to heal itself quickly, and therefore a water shortage is unlikely.

Is there anything else about the reduction in global population levels that you think we should know at this time?

Only that generations have been working on this for some time. It's not something they have suddenly thought about and are hurriedly trying to achieve. Many have been working on this from even thousands of years ago. Those who are interested in planning their destiny will have mapped out many incarnations to reach this point, often along with the rest of their soul group.

Normally how someone progresses in an individual life will change what they want to do next. But those that plan far ahead are usually pretty much past their own main growth on earth. They still have their own soul experiences, but they are more in control of those experiences, and are finishing off, and are there more for others.

life on a more highly evolved earth

SESSION 1

For those who remain here on earth, what will their experience be like?

Even we can't say. It's a new experience with this evolved body. We can estimate how many will awaken comfortably, and those who will fight it, and those who will put themselves in harm's way. Those who will be able to cope with it and those who can't. But we're watching with as much interest as you.

What actions should people take to change their vibration?

It will naturally happen as the vibration changes for those who choose to see not with their eyes.

Is there some way they can learn how to do that?

Humans never did quite learn. They always try too hard. Be like the animals, just let it happen. They know what's going on, they don't question.

Is there a way that an individual can influence what happens to them during this change?

Don't fight against the tide. You've already put everything into sequence in your life plan. All that's taking over is your consciousness of what you *think* you want to happen. Your soul already knows what's going to happen, so just let it happen. The key to everything is finding comfort and joy in change. Not to fight against it will be the most comfortable route, the path of nonresistance. Those who do resist will struggle, they'll be the ones who suffer, but it's not true suffering because they're just working on another experience.

As we move forward what's the most likely outcome for the global economy? Will human beings still need money?

Yes. Trade is always needed. No one person can provide everything for themselves. So trade is necessary, and money is a good vehicle for this. However the economy as we see it now will 'crash and burn' as you say. The international, global economy will collapse, and trade will be more local, so the same levels of bureaucracy will not be needed.

Is that definite?

It's not a definite, but it's the most likely outcome if the shifts and changes happen as we expect them to. There will be a lot less people living on the planet. The way people live will be so different, international exchange will not be necessary. It will shift and change and bend to what humans need, as has always been the case.

How will communities best organize themselves in the future?

People will naturally gravitate to others that they resonate with, and through that they will come up with their own plan as to the appropriate way to live. Some of the ways to live will be very similar to now. Others will find they understand more about themselves if they're closer to nature, and they will separate themselves off to do this.

Will there be any form of international travel?

Nothing is ruled out, nothing will completely stop. But the desire will be different. Desire drives humans in everything they do, so if the desire goes it will naturally recede. But nothing is impossible.

Are we planning to move away from duality here on earth?

There will always be a place for duality. The earth itself is set up in a way that life can only exist with some form of duality. But there will be more middle ground.

Less of the extremes?

Extremes were needed as a vehicle to take us to this place we're at now, but once the changes occur they won't be required.

SESSION 2

[At this point in the second session, having established that we needed to talk to a different energy about this topic, the new energy revealed that they were the second of the two we spoke to in the first session.]

Can you tell us anything more about what life will be like for those who continue to live on a more highly evolved earth?

As a whole it will be a wonderful time of great change. Yet it will only feel wonderful for those who can really embrace change and live in the present. There will be a period of serious disruption too, so it's inevitable that many people will find it very hard not to keep looking to the future and wondering what's going to happen next, and how they are going to cope. But those who can actually live in the present and enjoy these changes will progress in leaps and bounds.

Can we expect changes in people's thoughts and behavior and so on?

People will still believe what they believed before. But in terms of religion, for example, it will be as if they have discovered something new within that religion that they hadn't noticed before, which will allow them to accept what is happening more. This is something new and exciting, but it's only an add-on. Rather than throwing away the past they will be tuning into existing things they had not noticed or resonated with before, once they have greater understanding.

Can you comment again on whether we will be tending to live in smaller, more self-contained communities?

Yes, as things happen throughout the earth people will feel the need to move, they won't feel as safe as before. They will learn quickly that they need to listen to what's going on around them, and to their own intuition in terms of what is safe. So they will feel less compelled to live in places they are not comfortable with, and the changes will make it easier for them to move elsewhere.

For those who are not best suited to the city and to large towns things will become increasingly uncomfortable, as their minds start to expand with this new energy. Touching the minds of those around them when they don't resonate with them will be quite uncomfortable. So they will go to more remote areas, or at least make sure they join with others who are thinking similar thoughts.

An increasing number of cooperative spiritual communities are being planned even now. Will we see a lot more of these springing up?

There will be a need for these initially, there will be shortages of fuel and power, but it's simply a time of adaption, there will not be too much hardship. It will mean people need to go back to basics though, for a time. Then in the longer term there will be more what you might call eco-towns.

Will there be any particular parts of the world that will naturally attract those with lighter energies?

Places that aren't overly populated at the moment, simply because there will be more space and less need for struggle between the people there. There will be power struggles in places that are overpopulated already.

But no particular parts of the world that have been singled out as 'beacons of light' or anything like that?

Much has been said about these types of places, but the earth has pockets all over. Every place has its merits and its pros and cons, and if we were to point out any particular places there would be a convergence of people on them anyway. So people should merely feel where they are drawn to, even if it is on the other side of the world.

In the last session you said that those who resist the new energies will feel increasingly uncomfortable. Can you tell us more about that?

It will be similar to having a breakdown. They will be trying to hold on to what is familiar, particularly in terms of wealth and material things, and when these are either taken away or not bringing them as much comfort it will be a breakdown of sorts. A feeling of paranoia that other people are taking these from them. They simply will not have accepted that there could be any wealth other than the material, ignoring the wealth of the mind.

But they will still carry on existing in the new vibrations, they won't be wiped out by them?

It is their purpose to remain. Even though the duality will not be as extreme it will still be there, the earth cannot exist with only, as you would say, 'the positive'. There has to be a balancing of souls, even though that sounds quite cruel. As one vibration moves up there has to be another that goes denser.

Does that mean that the people not flowing with the shift are not less experienced souls, they're just experienced souls playing a different role?

They are generally quite experienced, yes. They are playing out the last parts of their earth experience, indeed the most difficult challenges they have chosen to date. But we're talking about such a small minority that it's not really balancing throughout, it's nowhere near as big as the number who will enjoy the experience.

Can you give us an idea of the percentage?

Five to ten, if that. But it might feel like there's more just because they will tend to be more explosive in their feelings.

But getting to this point will take time?

Yes.

What is your best estimate of when the major aspects of the energy shift will be complete?

By the year 2020 we will have seen the majority of change, and it should all be complete by about 2030.

We as individuals have been noticing the energies really shifting quickly of late, almost exponentially. Would that be right?

Yes. This is the best part for us watching, as more people actively notice and become aware of the energy rising. And as they share their experiences others wake up to it too. It is *so* exciting for us to see this rapid awakening taking place as planned.

On a separate note, because of the human tendency towards elitism and so on, I have a concern that people reading this may tend to hope they are one of those moving on to other places, rather than staying here on earth. Do you have any views on how that can be avoided, or do we just flow with it?

There will be a resonance for the right people, and it would be a good thing for them to start waking up to the possibility. Also, would it help if we told you that the souls on planet earth at the moment are the most evolved and ready they have ever been? People will enjoy reading that. This is one of the reasons why it was decided that an experiment could take place where the results were not already known. It is why the earth agreed for so many souls to incarnate, even though they could literally plunder it within an inch of its life.

We all hope, and even pray you might say, that you will all access at least tiny nuggets of your soul memories, and remember that you are having a full blown experience involving extremes of almost every emotion you've previously felt. And whether you are moving on from earth or staying, you are evolved to the extent that you can handle such change even while in an incarnate body. Even those who choose to stay and then live a life where they do not awaken to this energy are still incredibly experienced and evolved souls, relatively speaking.

So there aren't many new or inexperienced souls on earth at the moment?

A tiny number, a very tiny number. We did not want any new souls to be put off from having physical form by entering a life that was so extreme. There are a few, but that's only as a balance.

Is there anything else we need to know about life on a more evolved earth?

It will be a 'fuller' experience, that is the best way to describe it. It won't be so physical. People will spend more time in a type of meditation, just in terms of how they live their lives, which will enable them to interact with various types of energy to create a more complete experience.

So meditation is important?

It's something people will naturally do without even calling it meditation. Just focusing their mind on changing and shifting things will take it into a meditative state, which will actually be quite calming for the body. So there will be less diseases, less disorders of the body, it will be easier to keep their physical form in a healthy state. It will then be more likely that when people leave their bodies it will be at the time of their choosing, and this is more how it used to be before.

Rather than because of illness or ill-health you mean?

That will still play a part for some. But for most, when they have got to a point where they are ready, they will be able to choose to leave quite comfortably, while others around them will be more aware and will not hold them back.

Partly this will be because those left behind will be able to talk to their loved ones who have gone. Not quite as you would think, not full conversations, because that would just be confusing for all, and those who had departed would be tempted not to move on. But there will be an awareness and therefore a comfort. As a result people will be able to let go of the past more easily, and to live in the present. And once you can do that you can see the wonderful opportunities around you.

Presumably we will all still suffer from the ageing process, that won't go away?

It won't, but it will be somewhat slowed down. Someone who is older may look a lot younger than they do currently, because the physical form will be easier to look after and be better nourished physically and energetically. People will easily live to be one hundred and beyond.

Most of the people being born now have an evolved energy body. If tests were carried out you would see that their energy is quite different, and this will all help. And it has been going on for some time. Many are teenagers now, some even into their twenties, and their energy will act as a guiding light for many others who are struggling with the process. We have always known as incarnate souls to look to the wise and the elderly, and that will still partly be the case, but many will be looking at those who are younger because they will have brought more wisdom with them.

Does this also mean the veil of amnesia is being lowered for new souls coming in?

It is more that with this higher vibration they are more in tune with their higher self, and closer to it. They will still have amnesia about their past, but when they need information it will be easier for them to tap into it, and for it to come to them during meditation and sleep. And the more this happens the more it will be accepted, and they will not be seen as different or sick.

Is there anything else about them we would notice?

People will feel very comfortable around them. Those that don't are those on a slightly different path who will naturally gravitate elsewhere. But those going with the flow will naturally attune their energies to them, and this will be an easier process as their own energy opens up.

Will this be true of the majority of children born on earth from now on?

The majority, yes.

Does this mean both their physical body and their soul energy are more advanced?

There are some children even now who do not get sick any more, and that is because their physical body is more in tune with their energy body.

Presumably souls incarnating on earth in the future will still be on their soul journey, but it will just be a different kind of experience?

Yes. It's another variation and a fuller experience. Whereas before people may have been working on emotions, that won't be so important any more as their emotions won't be so extreme.

What sort of things will they be working on then?

They'll still be working on such things as relationships to the earth as well as to others, but it will also be about developing the new skill of expanding their energy out. This has been done before on a smaller scale, there have been many tribes where this was part of their culture, but never on such a global scale.

Can you explain more about this idea of expanding energy out?

It will be an experimental time. People will notice that once again they are able to do things with their minds. If they can remove fear they will find they can almost play with this new skill, and they will find how much it can help them. They will be able to project their minds to other places, for example to check for safety, or just to come into contact with other people, or to see what weather is coming. Whatever their choice of life they will find this new skill can be used in any area.

Will we be developing our telepathic abilities?

Some people will have a touching of minds where they can understand each other. But it will be more of a calling to someone, you would be able to think of them and they will think of you at the same time. You will know that you need to meet, or talk. That will be a skill that most people will be able to master relatively quickly.

Are we seeing this already?

Yes, and that's what people need to learn. This isn't something brand new, it's always been a possibility for some, it's just that the new energy coming through will allow *all* humans to do this. And it will be done more safely this time. The physical body will be more evolved so there will be a stronger tie that connects them when out of it, and it will be easier for them to reconnect after such an experience.

Why will this ability be important?

There will no longer be a need to travel to connect with people or see things, it will all be done on a different wavelength. People will be able to leave their body and meet up with other people, or go to see what is happening, or what weather is coming in. In other words they will be relying on their own natural resources rather than on technology to do such things.

And they will be fully conscious while doing it?

They can be, but some will choose not to be.

Can you talk about whether we will be introducing new forms of energy generation?

More and more people will be using the focus of their minds, so there will be a new technology that will harness the power of mind. However the majority of the forms of power that will be used are already here, even though many are only in their infancy.

Is there anything else you would like to say about the future of politics or of the global economy?

Whether you have wealth or not will make no difference after the shift. That's not to say be carefree with your money, it just means live in the present. Money and trade will always have a place, so it's common sense to keep some, and to surround yourself with a survival kit in terms of a home and food and so on. But long-term financial investments, for example, will be a thing of the past.

You're now seeing a new approach in the leaders coming through, in the freshness of their thinking, and in the people they use to advise them. They will be listening with more than just their ears. At this time of massive global change it is imperative that these leaders are highly evolved, so that they hold firm to their purpose and mission throughout. There are many in place already, and you will feel who these people are if you look at and listen to them with your heart, then you will know the truth. But they are still in a human body, so do not look to them to be perfect or never make mistakes.

[The following information was provided later in the second session by the excitable 'nature spirit' energy mentioned in the introduction.]

Can you tell us more about what life will be like for those going 'back to nature'?

I like the countryside! I like the ones who will be living in the countryside, they will be learning so much from the earth and from nature spirits. They will utilize nature a lot more, but not as now. They won't just use up the resources, they will actively give back to them as well. They will be able to influence the crops and everything living on the land with their minds to help it to grow. Especially after the shift, when they will need to grow crops quicker, they will find themselves using the energy from their hands and their minds. And getting together in communities will just speed this up even more.

There are some groups experimenting with this even now. And as more and more communities learn to do it they will share their knowledge as well, it will be a time of greater knowledge sharing.

Will you personally be helping this process?

Yes, I'm one of the ones who will help those in the countryside to learn to use the elements around them. I come from the elemental kingdom. And as the elementals or nature spirits progress through the energy cycles as well, they will be more inclined to work with humans rather than stay away from them. Humans might not realize it but they will be harnessing their help whenever they grow a crop, or freshen water, and so forth.

Can you tell us how people can get more in touch with elementals to work with them?

They're on a slightly different frequency and you need to be in tune with it. It's fair to say that the majority of humans are not sufficiently in tune to be able to contact them at this time, but even to have an awareness that they are around is very helpful. And give them respect, they respond to respect.

So just asking respectfully for their help?

Yes, even if you can't see them. The more the energy within people is raised and the frequency changes, the more they will be able to interact with some of these nature spirits, although different people tend to be more in tune with one type of elemental than another.

our ability to accelerate the process

SESSION 1

What can we do to help the process?

Awaken others. You've chosen to awaken early, which is a hard path, which is why we help you so much along the way. But where you're in the minority now, very soon you won't be. More and more people every day are becoming more and more aware, and that is the main role you play, in helping this.

Helping people to accept the concept of their soul living on after death?

Fear of change is the biggest obstacle. And bringing the longevity of their soul to people's awareness will help the expansion of the mind, but cannot be done if there is fear in place.

What's the best medium for us to help more people to understand this?

Through your own increased vibration. This is not intellect we're talking about. People resonate with vibrations, and those who are willing and open to new understanding will resonate and find the right people. It's not what you say, it's not even what you teach, it's what you give out on a vibrational level they will pick up.

What is useful for us to be putting in place at this time?

Possibilities. Giving people opportunities to see what's before them and to decide if they choose to think of these things fully now, or just open their eyes a bit for later. Possibilities are the greatest vehicle for us all to learn and grow, and to choose and change our experience.

SESSION 2

[Although some of these messages are more personally directed they have been included because they have a far broader applicability than just to ourselves.]

Apart from flowing with things, and meditating, is there any other advice you can give us about how we can assist the energy shift in ourselves as individuals?

As we start opening up our minds and discovering new talents, instead of them becoming an energy block within our system that we don't understand, our awareness will enable us to see where we can go with these energies, how they can work for us. This is the opening up of the mind that we talked about previously. There are many exercises for all this out there already, but using the ones that are easiest and simplest to remember will best ensure that people carry them out.

Are there any in particular that you would like to share with us now?

Simply for people to discover their own way to tune into their inner self, to go within before going outwards, in whatever way they resonate with. So meditation, as you say, and other simple techniques to go inside. But everyone is so different, that is why they need to discover their own technique for this.

Apart from meditation is there anything else we can do to open ourselves up to messages from our higher self or spirit guides?

Sound is very important. Different sounds resonate with different people. Music in particular will resonate with particular energy sites within the body, and so people should try to find music that enables them to go inside themselves.

Can that be any kind of music?

Certainly, and it will vary at different times in our lives, and depending on what we're going through. Also for many with very busy lives who are not set up to think too much about such things, mediums such as television, films, books and other sources will be enough to open them up, and remind them at the correct time that there may be other possibilities.

If we switch now to how we can help others to wake up to the shift, will the broader use of regression and other therapy also have a significant role?

Yes, it's another way that people can reconnect with their souls. Anything that helps them to do that will be on the increase.

But was it always foreseen that at this time there would be more people doing this kind of work?

We originally thought there would be a huge number of souls, helping each other to come through all this together. When we realized this was not happening quite as much as we expected, with more conflict between people, some souls agreed to switch into a slightly different role to do this work. For some this wasn't in their original plan but it was renegotiated because their purpose was all about the soul growth of others, so they knew their contracts might change along the way.

You said in the last session that it's not what we say or write so much as the vibrations we give off that will be most important. Have you anything to add to that?

What you say or write is important, but it's the energy behind it that really matters. Two people can be teaching the same thing, but if one has an underlying energy of optimism, and love not fear, that will be picked up. If another teaches the same thing without this energy they will be less effective at waking people up.

So writing books and giving lectures and so on is still important?

Very important. But so is the energy behind it, and what we are doing now is an important vehicle to release that positive energy. It is also why we as a council are involved at this time. We would not be giving these messages if they were only to be heard by a few people. As much as we are happy to do that, it is important for many people to hear this, especially people who are struggling and looking for something that resonates with them that they have not yet found.

So is there anything we need to be aware of in terms of making sure this message gets to as many people as need it?

There will be many unseen helpers. But also don't forget that this is not simply a book, your purposes are entwined with these messages and you will all be speaking to people about them, giving lectures and so on, so the book is only part of it. And other people will pick up on them and start talking about them too, creating a real energy and excitement behind them.

How important is this work compared, for example, to our therapy work?

Each has its role. Many people will sort themselves out and shift things without being drawn to a therapist, so entertaining books and talks and documentaries will also help them to wake up.

It has been suggested that, rather than concentrating specifically on helping others, if we concentrate on our own growth, openness and happiness, the rest will just come. Is that correct?

That will help you to help others *so much*. This is still a time of people's own soul growth and enjoyment – remember this must be for enjoyment. So you should go to wherever you will be happiest, not where you think you will help the most people, because wherever you are you will attract those you need to help. The more you can be what some who are not so in tune may even perceive as selfish, the better. There will be work wherever you go, and the more you are in places where you want to be and are happy, the lighter your own vibration will be and the more people and souls and consciousnesses you will attract and help.

Remember it's not just those you can see, you are giving this help in lots of different ways. Even with those people you only momentarily come into contact with, if it is their time to release certain elements, whether energies of their own or spirit attachments or whatever, sometimes your higher vibration will allow them to do this. So do not think you are ever being selfish.

What about people helping to clear the earth's own energy field?

Although it is not really the right word, there are large areas that need to be cleared of intense 'negative' energies trapped in the earth, which can still affect people's energy systems. There are a number of people doing this.

[At this point in the session the excitable 'nature spirit' energy mentioned in the introduction was so keen to talk to us he spontaneously took over.]

Is there anything else we need to know about the ways we can accelerate this process, whether in ourselves or others?

Be who you were born to be! There are so many wonderful souls here now who are in tune with themselves, and with us too. So shine that light! If you could look at all the souls now, as they really are with their light shining out, it's like fireflies at night. It's brilliant to watch from a distance as you look down and see all the people opening up! It's just so exciting, there's so many more people who are awake than you think! You can see them, I watch them at night, their night time, and it's my job to see where they still have some denseness and blockages. But these are getting less and less. It's wonderful, I can go through whole swathes of people and know that they can release what they need to on their own from now on.

More and more people are awakening through every medium, this whole global shift is wonderful because it speeds everything up. The things people are seeing on television – isn't television wonderful! – and films, they have so many experiences, and virtual experiences, they get to understand and remember what it's like not to have physical form. And it's so much easier for them to open up than it's ever been.

why everything is as it should be

SESSION 1

What's the purpose of the negative media hype about 2012?

No experience is worthwhile if it's easy. The role of almost half the souls here is to bring conflict in, to obscure what people start to see. And the energy that is created in overcoming these obstacles, and in changing awareness, is what's helping the planet itself to evolve and grow.

The earth agreed to have so many souls incarnate on its back for this period as that's helping it to evolve too. Humanity's parasitic nature is helping the earth to break free of its bonds, to increase its own vibrational level. So the things you see as bad that people have done to the planet are purely them fulfilling a soul-to-earth contract. To help it grow and do what it needs to vibrate out, to start moving up and shifting its own vibration. So everything you can think of is just a beautiful play that has an end in sight, and every character has to play their part to reach that end.

Do events like Haiti help people to wake up to who they are?

When someone sees what can happen in an instant to another human being, not only do they have compassion but they think about their own life, they think how quickly change can happen. And that in itself brings about awareness, and starts to loosen their whole bond with what they felt was the permanent nature of the world around them. They start to understand that change can happen in an instant. But they're also opening up to the fact that change can be for good as well as bad.

SESSION 2

We talked in the last session about the massively increased population and its pollution acting like a parasite on the back of the planet, which will in fact help it to raise its vibrations. Can we discuss that a little more now?

Yes, everything that is being done to the earth at present that you tend to see as bad, for example taking its resources, will ultimately just enable it to fight back with a survival instinct similar to your own. It's calling on energy that it hasn't needed for quite some time to bring that back. There are people trying to help it now, and it's not that their efforts are futile, but the whole raising of consciousness will, in its own right, give the earth what it needs. As more people become aware of the shift, without realizing it they are energetically helping the earth, they are putting their emotions and energy into it, which will help the process.

So the earth is behaving just as we are, in that we all have to face obstacles to raise our energy levels so that we properly resonate with the shift. Is that correct?

Yes. And the earth is calling in resources it hasn't needed for a long time. Mining is particularly important. Over the last few hundred years this has depleted so many resources deep within the earth that it needs to make drastic changes and literally push its energy outwards.

We have a concern that this might be misinterpreted by some as meaning they don't have to care about the pollution of the earth, but we suspect this is not what you intend at all. Can you clarify that for us?

What you are telling them are truths they learned before birth, and they will wake up to that. For those whose path is to pollute the earth, when they read these messages they will regard it as justification to carry on, and this is what we need, it's all part of the increase in energy levels. For those whose mission is to save the earth, they will become angered by this behavior and try even harder, and more of their emotions will be poured into her. These messages will resonate with everyone at a soul level and will only amplify what they are already doing, which can only be a good thing. This is an amazing time, people are living and fulfilling their soul purpose. They need to be empowered with these messages to remove their fear.

Is the message still very much that everything is just as it should be?

Very much so, and if something is missing things will be set in motion that will help it to manifest. We learn as we go along as well, nothing is set in stone. As things change we adapt just like you adapt. So at this very moment in time everything is perfect. Even if things might be perceived to be wicked or evil or other such words that are often used, nothing has been corrupted, and that is a significant difference from last time.

Are there really any forces or entities that can be thought of as negative or operating 'outside the plan'?

There is negative but nothing outside of the plan, as with any environment that has duality. Even the council has both negative and positive if you want to use those terms, and it is the soul memories of these things that are deep within us that have given rise to the references to all this found in various religions. They all have gods and devils, heavens and hells, that's simply the dualistic perception of it all. But this darker side is just as needed in the world.

So nothing is outside of the plan?

No.

And there are no 'demonic forces' trying to 'subvert the course of righteousness'?

People who suggest that are fighting their own battle. They resonate with it because they have their own inner struggle with opposing forces, and they are projecting it onto something else.

So they are externalizing something that is really internal?

Yes.

universal excitement over this unique opportunity

SESSION 1

Is this the first time this kind of opportunity has ever arisen in the history of the universe?

It's difficult to explain, because it's not the first time, but for the vibration or level that we all work on it is. There are different changes on different scales going on the whole time. But this, even in our eyes, is on a very grand scale.

What's the purpose of not having a certain outcome this time round?

New experiences will be born out of it that even we haven't conceived yet. The spiritual awakening that is happening globally is like a baby opening its eyes for the first time. We decided this time to give a glimpse of eternity to people. This is one of the reasons why it's so exciting at this time. Never before have you had the chance to be in a body but also see eternity. How amazing that is!

And we are watching to see how this will help you to grow and shift without people using it in a way that is wasn't meant for. This is why we're so excited this time round. It's not by chance that you can now see what you can see. We know that this is necessary for the changes that need to be put into place, so that the veil of fear can be lifted for the majority rather than the minority.

Do you have any final messages for us?

When you can see past what goes on immediately around you, the excitement for change is incredible! If you could feel what we feel! It is exciting for us to be able to be involved, and to be heard in your lives. This is a first. This we did not do the last time, and we're learning from it. And your group is just one of many. This is happening all over. And if we can instill anything in you it's the excitement of the culmination of this process, of why you have chosen to be here.

SESSION 2

Do you have any further positive messages that will reinforce our sense of excitement about this unique opportunity?

You may think of the earth like a caterpillar. All this time it's been growing, and for the last few thousand years it's almost like it's been in a cocoon, while all these souls have been playing out their roles on it. And now a butterfly is emerging. That is the best way to think of how the earth will be after the shift. This beautiful thing.

And just like the caterpillar couldn't fly before and now it can, this energy will bring through new qualities, new things that can be done, new experiences, the earth will have another dimension to it. And the people on it will experience that dimension. There will be better communication. There will be better understanding. It will be a more gentle place to live. Duality will still remain but people will be more comfortable with the middle ground.

Do you have any more final messages for us?

Many of you have waited many, many years and even lifetimes to get to this point. And it's a shame that so many of you have waited so long, and yet now you're nearly there you don't have the excitement and enthusiasm, but have fear instead. The most important thing to remember is that you have chosen this because it is an incredible journey! And an expansion you would not have experienced in a physical body before, or at least not for a very long time.

So these are exciting possibilities that we should be looking forward to...

YES!

JANET TRELOAR saw and communicated with spirits from an early age. She chose to repress this natural ability as she got older but, after many years working in the corporate sector, various synchronicities led her to rediscover it. Now as a graduate of the PLRA she has a private regression therapy practice operating out of Woodford Green and Central London, with spirit release work as one of her specialisms. This is her first major foray into channeling, and she is now undertaking further research on 2012 with Tracey. She also hopes to emigrate to Vancouver at some stage to set up a PLRA affiliated regression training centre. For more information see *www.planet-therapies.com*.

HAZEL NEWTON is the co-director of the PLRA. She has a private regression therapy practice in Bristol, specializing in soul contracts and healing the inner child. She also runs basic and advanced hypnosis classes, is currently co-authoring a book to be called *Rational Reincarnation* with Peter Jenkins and Toni Ann Winninger, and writes a monthly column for *www.mastersofthespiritworld.com*. For more information see *www.radiantsouls.co.uk*.

TRACEY ROBINS was born in Melbourne, Australia and is privileged to have traveled widely. As a graduate of the PLRA she has established a private regression therapy practice in Manchester. She is currently undertaking further research on 2012 with Janet, and hopes to return to Australia at some stage to set up a PLRA affiliated regression training centre. For more information see *www.lifecycletherapies.com*.

THE HISTORY OF THE SOUL
fallen angels, forgotten ancestors and karmic catastrophes

by Ian Lawton

Rational Spirituality Press, 2010
www.rspress.org

'A dramatic new vision of the origins of civilization, born out of a profound understanding of ancient spirituality.' Andrew Collins, revisionist author

Was our planet once populated by a lost civilization that was destroyed? A fundamental reappraisal of the most revered ancient texts and traditions from around the globe, coupled with archaeological and geological evidence, suggests that it was. But what were our antediluvian ancestors like? Rather than huddling in caves to escape the ice age, were they expert navigators and astronomers who traveled far and wide? And did they have access to incredible technology, or was their culture defined far more by its spirituality?

Indeed, what was it that caused the massive surge in culture that began around 75,000 years ago and led directly to the evolution of the modern human race? What ongoing impetus allowed it to snowball so rapidly, compared to the slow but steady evolution of our hominid forebears over millions of years? Were divine sages really sent to introduce civilization to humanity, and if so how can we understand who or what they really were? Some sort of gods, or extraterrestrial visitors? Or were they just highly experienced souls incarnating on earth with a job to do, as they still do?

Is there evidence that our forgotten ancestors were almost completely wiped out? If so, how did this happen, and when? And was it just a random natural catastrophe, or was there an underlying 'karmic dynamic' related to their increasing preoccupation with the material at the expense of the spiritual? Most important of all, did their destruction have anything to do with universal energetic cycles? And, if so, what can we learn about the future we now face in the modern era? Are we once again surfing the crest of a huge energetic wave?

The veiled pointers to our hidden past have finally been unmasked as more than just the psychological constructs of philosophically primitive cultures. History is repeating itself. But what will happen this time round? And is the script already written... or can our actions now still help to dictate the outcome?

THE WISDOM OF THE SOUL
profound insights from the life between lives
by Ian Lawton *with* Andy Tomlinson

Rational Spirituality Press, 2007

www.rspress.org

'This fine book provides much-needed information about everything from trapped spirits to demonic beings; from the purpose of incarnation to extraterrestrial realms; and from legends of Atlantis to global warming and humanity's future. I cannot recommend it highly enough.' Edith Fiore, pioneering regression therapist and author of *You Have Been Here Before*

'The research in this book poses questions that have rarely, if ever, been asked before.' Hans TenDam, pioneering regression therapist and author of *Exploring Reincarnation*

For thousands of years our view of the afterlife has been handed down to us by a variety of prophets and gurus
But in the last few decades thousands of ordinary people have been taken back into their 'life between lives' in the light realms
Their consistent reports form one of the most profound sources of spiritual wisdom ever available to humanity
And now two researchers have decided to push this source to its limits...

It is important enough that we should understand what happens to us between lives in the light realms: how we receive energy healing to lighten our vibrations; how we review our lives without judgment from higher beings; and how we choose and plan our next lives along with close soul mates, in order to face the lessons and experiences that will most allow us to grow.

But what if we could use the interlife experience to answer a host of more universal questions of spiritual, historical and philosophical importance? About everything from unusual soul behavior and soul development, through humanity's past and future, to the true nature of reality and time? What if multiple regression subjects came up with consistent answers? And what if they displayed wisdom so profound as to be way beyond any normal human capacity?

THE BIG BOOK OF THE SOUL
Rational Spirituality for the twenty-first century

by Ian Lawton

Rational Spirituality Press, 2008
www.rspress.org

'I predict that the author's proposal of a holographic model of the soul will be one of the most important concepts of our time.' Hans TenDam, pioneering regression therapist and author of *Exploring Reincarnation*

'This book is filled with thorough reviews of research and thoughtful analysis of its implications. It makes a significant contribution to the field. I recommend it highly.' Jim Tucker, University of Virginia Division of Perceptual Studies and author of *Life Before Life*

'This fine book is masterly and scholarly.' Edith Fiore, pioneering regression therapist and author of *You Have Been Here Before*

Rational spirituality... surely this is a contradiction in terms?
How can spirituality be rational, when it relies on faith and revelation?
The simple answer is it does not have to any more...

There is persuasive evidence from near-death and out-of-body experiences that the physical brain is merely the instrument through which our soul consciousness expresses itself in the physical world. There is equally persuasive evidence from children who remember past lives, and from past-life and interlife regression, that we are individual souls who reincarnate to experience and grow.

A careful analysis of skeptics' arguments in each of these areas of research proves in most cases just how reductionist, and in fact illogical, they are. Nevertheless not all the evidence put forward by believers stands up, and careful discrimination is required. Such a balanced and in-depth critique of both sides of the argument is rare if not unique. Equally unique is the accompanying collation and comparison of the interlife regression research of a number of pioneering psychologists.

But what of the idea that 'we are all One', which is the universal message of all transcendental experiences? Can it be squared with the idea of the individual, reincarnating soul, or is this merely an 'illusion' in itself? Perhaps the answer lies in a theory of total elegance and simplicity... that of the holographic soul.

IAN LAWTON was born in 1959. In his mid-thirties he became a writer-researcher specializing in ancient history, esoterica and spiritual philosophy. His first two books, *Giza: The Truth* (1999) and *Genesis Unveiled* (2003), have sold over 30,000 copies worldwide.

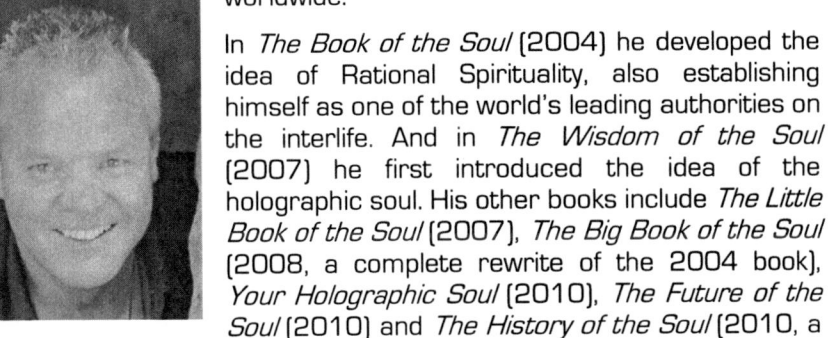

In *The Book of the Soul* (2004) he developed the idea of Rational Spirituality, also establishing himself as one of the world's leading authorities on the interlife. And in *The Wisdom of the Soul* (2007) he first introduced the idea of the holographic soul. His other books include *The Little Book of the Soul* (2007), *The Big Book of the Soul* (2008, a complete rewrite of the 2004 book), *Your Holographic Soul* (2010), *The Future of the Soul* (2010) and *The History of the Soul* (2010, a revision of the 2003 book).

He is also a practicing current, past and between life regression therapist. For further information see *www.ianlawton.com*.